THE ART DEC
A Guide

To Richard
My Passepartout

ART DECO TRAVELLER

A Guide to Britain

Genista Davidson

Published by Art Deco Publisher, 2015
Printed by Barkers Print & Design Ltd

First published in 2015
by Art Deco Publishers
Kemp House, 152 City Road, LONDON EC1V 2NX
artdeco-traveller.co.uk

ISBN 978-0-9934146-0-2

Art Deco Traveller ®

Printed and bound in Great Britain by Barkers Print & Design Ltd
Attleborough, Norfolk NR17 2NP

Preparation for your Travels

Luggage - If you want to make your sojourn as authentic as possible, lose that pull along suitcase and opt for something more in style with the period. You can easily purchase period suitcases in various conditions in vintage shops or online auctions, and these will not break the bank, even though they may break your back! If you are driving door to door this should cause no discomfort, but when crossing London Underground, they do cause some arm ache (I speak from experience here!). I do assure you though that it will enhance your trip as you step back in time.

If travelling by car, whilst en route listen to chart toppers of the thirties which are readily available via all media (yes, the wonders of modern day technology!)

You may not specifically be interested in the fashion of the time, but again, it will enhance your whole experience. If you incorporate only a little authentic clothing or accessories, the overall ambiance will alter. This may be an original pretty hankerchief slipped in your handbag or into the gentleman's pocket. A neat little 1930s handbag or silk scarf, will add that sense of nostalgia. Of course you can get wonderfully reproduced clothes in the period style which will be just as wonderful for you, or you can spend a near fortune on getting all original items which can take time and energy sourcing, only to find out that they are far to fragile to actually wear. You will need to do your research on this area and inevitably learn by 'trial and error'.

A wonderful book for reference is *1930s Fashion The Definitive Sourcebook,* edited by Charlotte Fiell & Emmanuelle Dirix. This colourful informative Bible is a must for all 30s Fashionistas. Likewise another book I fully recommend is *Art Deco Fashion* by Suzanne Lussier, a V&A Publication. This fascinating book takes the reader through the Period and its Designers, and showcases some evocative costumes.

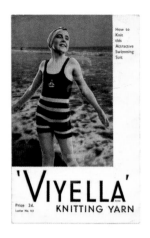

How to Knit this Attractive Swimming Suit

'VIYELLA'

Price 2d.

KNITTING YARN

If you are a keen knitter perhaps you would like to parade on the beach in your homemade swimsuit.

I recommend the non itchy wool and I have three delightful knitted swimsuits which get regular wear, much to Jeeves' raised eyebrows!

Popular flowers of the time were subtle shades of roses in buttery ivories or soft pinks, lillies and dahlias. Why not request a vase prior to arrival or have the pleasure is choosing your own from a nearby florist on the day of your arrival.

No art deco escapade would be complete without taking your best writing pen (I prefer a fountain pen for the sheer joy of feeling the ink flow onto the page). If the hotel has writing paper, use it! I have for many years written to my dear Aunt Mary, now entering her nonagenarian years, and she relishes receiving the embossed quality sheets, emailing me back to thank me, and advising me that she is looking forward to the next instalment.

I then seek out quality authentic post cards to update my family and friends on my newest travels. Popping the cards in the post box fills me with bygone memories.

THE MIDLAND HOTEL, MORECAMBE.

CONTENTS

Preparing for your Travels ....v - vi

How to use this Book viii

The following Chapters have sub-sections on:
Accommodation, Restaurants, Bars & Cafes,
Theatres & Cinemas, Lidos, Points of Interest

LONDON 9

SOUTH EAST 77

SOUTH WEST 113

EAST MIDLANDS 148

WEST MIDLANDS 164

NORTH EAST 179

NORTH WEST 195

SCOTLAND 215

WALES 237

Credits & Acknowledgements 248

Modern Revival of the Jazz Age 249

Saving our Art Deco Heritage 251

Index ....252 - 259

How to Use this Book

The book covers 9 geographical areas in Britain. Each area has 5 sections including accommodation which covers hotels, bed & breakfasts and self catering. I have not included prices as these will always vary depending when and where you book the accommodation.

Please telephone or email the premises prior to attending to ensure that details are correct at that time to avoid disappointment. Over the years I have been caught out by going to visit a well know art deco premises, only to find out it has subsequently closed or been revamped into a different outlet. Many of the hotels have independent restaurants which are open to non-residents so there are cross references in the restaurants and bars section.

When visiting lidos always check prior to attending. Depending on weather and other conditions out of their control, they may have to close without much notice. Also, please bear in mind that not all the premises or interiors are original art deco. It may be in the 'style' of art deco or have influences of art deco, some of which is modern day contemporary, so please do check via websites or in person as to whether it will be what you are expecting.

I have visited many other buildings and accommodation over the years which have leanings towards Art Deco but I do not have the space to include them all so my sincere apologies for any omissions. Most of all I do hope you enjoy your art deco travels and when travelling always remember that 'the glass is half full' never 'half empty'.

'The world is a book and those who do not
travel read only one page.'
Augustine of Hippo

LONDON

Accommodation	10
Restaurants, Bars & Cafes	31
Theatres & Cinemas	55
Lidos	62
Places of Interest	68

LONDON ACCOMMODATION

An Art Deco hotel evokes a nostalgic time when a new modern age was dawning, the excitemen and glamour you experience when lounging around the hotel's public spaces, dining in the opulen restaurants, or sipping a cocktail in one of the stunning bars, creates a feeling like no other.

London's gorgeous art deco hotels, may be expensive, but well worth every penny. When bookin, I recommend that you specifically ask for an Art Deco Room or at least a room which incorporate some of this style, but with many of the hotels it is the architectural building and public areas whic display the art deco features, and not necessary the bedrooms. Most of these hotels offer afternoo tea, so even if you are not spending the night at the hotel, you can still enjoy the sumptuou surroundings. Alternatively, you do not necessarily need to stay overnight. Depending on you agenda you can book for lunch, dinner or just enjoy a relaxing drink in the bar.

Please contact the hotels directly for tariffs, either looking on their websites or by using the man hotel comparison sites. I have not included prices as these fluctuate according to season an special offers. Please be aware that some of the London hotels do have strict dress code (whic means you are never overdressed), so please check this out before you arrive.

It is also worth knowing that many of London's four and five star hotels have now updated to contemporary modern new look, not unlike the art deco interior designs of yesteryear. You wi find that the Baglioni Hotel on Hyde Park Gate SW7 has beautiful décor incorporating straigh lines, asymmetrically pleasing chrome and black bathrooms and a decadent foyer of bold gold an shining chandeliers.

The Alywych Hotel, Aldwych WC2 is also one to mention, as the contemporary feel to this hote also transports you back to those 'heady' days. The luxurious surroundings with original art wor and clean cut décor are so complimentary to the building. If you are on a tight budget The Princ Regent Hotel 361-363 Prince Regent Lane, London E16 3JP Phone: 020 7474 222 www.princeregent-hotel.com which has 34 rooms is a very reasonably priced 3 star hotel that ha an original art deco exterior.

What follows are the grande dames in art deco, the ones to spend time in and enjoy the individually unique architecture and fine examples of original deco ornaments and features.

Claridge's Hotel

49 Brook Street, London WIK 4HR Tel: 020 7629 8860 www.claridges.co.uk

Claridge's has 197 rooms including 62 suites. During the late 1920s when London's bright young things were partying like no other, Claridge's invited art deco pioneer Basil Lonides to modernise the restaurant and several suites. His magnificent engraved glass screens still adorn the restaurant today.

By 1929 the hotel was a world-renowned showcase for top British designers. Oswald Milne designed a new main entrance, and a façade of Roman stone and jazz moderne mirrored foyer completed Claridge's new look.

The grand success of the art deco redesign inspired a much larger project. In the early 1930s Milne added an extension to the east side of Claridge's. With its simple cubic outline, the tall brick block stands in both contrast to and harmony with the main hotel building.

Inside, Milne created a fine suite of reception rooms and guestrooms furnished with smart, eclectic style. The bold lines and sweeping curves of the style give Claridge's its unmistakable air of timeless elegance

This hotel truly is one of London's most glamorous and it astonishes your senses from the moment you step inside. The splendid zig-zag design mirror and wall light fitting along with a leaping deer palique glass lamp and foliage in the lobby, engulf you as you glide in.

The beautifully appointed one-bedroom Deluxe Mayfair Suites, with pretty period details, mirrored powder rooms and a fantastic layout, certainly will not disappoint. The Linley Suite with deco-style interiors by the royal furniture-maker, is a gem, as is the Brooke Suite; but then no room will disappoint.

The joy of relaxing in the public areas and partaking of a cocktail served in Lalique crystal in the 1930s themed Fumoir bar just makes your heart skip a beat; life does not get much better than this

The French Salon has original Art Deco features such as the ironwork tassels also by Basil Ionide and winged Renaissance-style cherubs above the doors. It features a striking mural of a dancing couple, discovered when the room was being refurbished. This Hotel is pure escapism, and will transport you back to another time, but of course has the modern day technology should you require it. You certainly will not feel out of place in your glamorous frock and stylish cravat here.

The Dorchester

Park Lane, Mayfair, London W1K1QA
Tel: 0207 629 8888 www.dorchestercollection.com Opened 1931

The Dorchester offers accommodation of exceptional grace and comfort, all suites providing either Hyde Park or city views.

The luxury suites range in size from the Junior and Stanhope Suites to the generous Dorchester Suites and the famous Oliver Messel Suite.

Bathrooms are welcoming and spacious, offering an exceptional combination of style and function and are said to have the deepest baths in London. They are predominantly made of Italian marble and designed in the classic art deco style - echoing the hotel's 1930s origins.

The Dorchester Bar was rebuilt in 1938. Harry Craddock, one of the most famous barmen at the time, produced three of the most popular cocktails of the day - the Martini, Manhattan and White Lady - and sealed them in phials, which were set into the wall of the bar 'for posterity'. When the bar was reconstructed in 1979, the cocktails, scroll and recipes were found to be in excellent condition.

The Dorchester combines iconic British style, with a contemporary 'take' of the 1930s Art Deco glamour. Royalty and political leaders, both British and foreign, have been frequent visitors. Princess Elizabeth, the present Queen, attended a dinner party at The Dorchester the day before her engagement was announced on 10th July 1947, and it was here that Prince Philip celebrated his stag night on the eve of his wedding. The list of visitors to The Dorchester from the entertainment

world is of prodigious length. To name but a few: Danny Kaye, who originally appeared in cabaret at the hotel for £50.00 a week in the 1930s, became a lifelong regular guest... as did Elizabeth Taylor always occupying a suite, Sir Ralph Richardson, who tended to arrive by motorcycle, and Alfred Hitchcock. You can unwind in the glamorous Art Deco relaxation room before heading to The Spatisserie for a glass of champagne. Even the new China Tang restaurant at the Dorchester was designed with Art Deco touches.

The May Fair

Stratton Street, Mayfair, London W1J 8LT
0207 769 8200 www.themayfairhotel.co.uk Opened 1927

This historic hotel with a modern interior design, is set in the very heart of Mayfair, London. It was first opened by King George V and has played host to some of London's most extravagant society

events. The May Fair claims that the stylish rooms have hosted many intimate liaisons: the risqué, the scandalous and the happily married and that adventures of the heart, meetings of the mind, tales of whisky-soaked raconteurs, gatherings of nighthawks and earlybirds are all welcome. Celebrations in white and carpets in red...life's dramas played out on London's legendary stage. The May Fair has been home to lavish suites, glamorous bars and affairs since 1927.

The Schiparelli suite is unmistakable, with an opulent flamboyant style. The spirit of surrounding Mayfair is captured beautifully, especially in the May Fair bar, breathtaking Crystal Room and opulent Danziger Suite.

The exclusive enclave, the cigar room at the heart of the hotel recreates the outdoors and is encased in a striking stainless steel mesh that lets the space 'breathe'. It conjures up pictures of 'Those Wild Young Things'.

This Hotel just oozes the roaring 20s whilst cavorting with the 21st century. You really feel that you have just walked off the set of 'The Great Gatsby'.

The Cigar Room

The Savoy Hotel

Strand, London WC2R 0EU 020 7836 4343

The Savoy Hotel provides the glamour of yesteryear with the functionality of today. Originally opened in 1889 the hotel has made its place in history, hosting royalty, world leaders and legend of the stage and screen It truly is one of the world's iconic hotels and you feel as if you are one of the leading lights in the cast of a Metro-Goldwyn-Mayer film as you enter this establishment.

You are greeted by the statue of Count Peter by Frank Lynn Jenkins, which has been likened to the Rolls Royce 'spirit of ecstasy' mascot above the stainless steel canopy which was designed by architects Easton & Robertson, during the hotels redecoration by Basil Ionides in 1926-29.

he style and glamour, honouring the hotel's two main aesthetics, English Edwardian and Art Deco, exceptional in the guestrooms and suites. It seamlessly blends the traditional with discreet echnology. Each of the 195 guest-rooms and 73 suites are decorated in either Edwardian or Art eco style, and many afford breath-taking views over the River Thames. The suites take inspiration om high profile guests, while the two-bedroom Royal Suite is an impressive stately procession of ooms spread across the front of the entire fifth floor, overlooking the river.

esigner, Pierre Yves Rochon has used the finest materials – from Murano glass chandeliers and k wall coverings to Italian linens and marble floors. No two rooms or suites are the same and any have original features.

Kaspar's Seafood Bar and Grill

One of the most exciting restaurant launches in The Savoy's 124 year old illustrious history, Kaspar Seafood Bar and Grill offers an informal yet luxury dining experience in an elegant 1920s style.

The American Bar is a luxury classic bar. The Cocktail list combines the finest drinks of the past with innovative new twists.

The Savoy also has an impressive rooftop swimming pool - so don't forget to pack that 1930's inspired swim suit.

Beaufort B

Also, look out for Kaspar the Cat, a beautiful art deco sculpture created to ward off bad luck and please ask the staff the story behind it.

Strand Palace Hotel

372 Strand, London WC2R 0JJ 020 7379 4737 www.strandpalacehotel.co.uk

his was once one of London's most glamorous Art Deco buildings and has now been completely pdated. It is an iconic building which is perfectly placed if your London visit is about theatres, ightseeing and nightlife. The Strand Palace Hotel has a fascinating history dating back to 1907, when permission was granted to build a 'grand' hotel in the prominent Westminster thoroughfare of the Strand. Two years later, the hotel opened for business. At that time, a single room with reakfast would have set you back five shillings and six pence – 27p in today's money.

As London roared into the Twenties, the adjoining Haxell's Hotel was acquired in order to expan
and modernise the Strand Palace. Art Deco features were incorporated into many of the publi
areas, and the Hotel became a popular venue for social gatherings, where London's best an
brightest could show off their dancing skills with displays of the Charleston and Tango.

Some of the original Art Deco architecture can still be seen today in the historic facade, and th
property has been featured in several movies and television period dramas.

The Wellesley

11 Knightsbridge, London SW1X 7LY 020 7235 3535 www.thewellesley.co.uk

The Wellesley has contemporary luxury, art deco glamour and uncompromising service i
Knightsbridge, London.

Each of the 36 suites and bedrooms is individually finished with sumptuous décor and amenitie
The jewel in the crown is the Wellesley Penthouse, overlooking Hyde Park, which occupies th
entire sixth and seventh floors.

The Jazz Lounge echoes to the spirit of legends who have graced this building. The Crystal Ba
and Oval Restaurant celebrate the 1920s, all glamour and style.

The elegance of the décor, the sounds and the ambience recall another era.

The Beaumont

Balderton Street, Mayfair, London WIK 6TF 020 7499 1001 www.thebeaumont.com

With just 50 rooms, 13 studios and 10 suites, The Beaumont occupies a historic 1926 building overlooking Brown Hart Gardens. Classic, restrained elegance are the hallmark of the rooms and suites at The Beaumont. Floor-to-ceiling sliding doors shut the rooms off from the generous, private entrance halls and bathrooms. The finest finishes, including high-gloss rosewoods, bronze mirroring, chagrin detailing and generous pale silks are used throughout. The beds and linens are supremely comfortable. Original paintings and photographs of the period, collected from all over the world, adorn the walls.

There are a number of dining options at The Beaumont, including The American Bar and The Colony Grill Room. The Cub Room is a private bar and lounge, for the exclusive use of hotel residents and their visitors.

The Ritz London

150 Piccadilly, London W1J 9BR 020 7493 8181 www.theritzlondon.com

The Ritz London owes its architectural design to the successful partnership formed in 1900 between Frenchman Charles Mewés and Englishman Arthur Davis and was opened in 1906.

Throughout its 110 year history The Ritz has attracted the famous and the fashionable. During its early years, the hotel enjoyed the patronage of The Prince of Wales, later to become King Edward VIII, and the English aristocracy. King Alfonso of Spain and Queen Amelie of Portugal met in the hotel; Pavlova, the Russian Prima Ballerina, danced at The Ritz; the Aga Khan and Paul Getty had suites; and Churchill, de Gaulle

and Eisenhower met for summit meetings in the Marie Antoinette Suite during the Second World War. The Ritz also became the favourite of Hollywood stars; Charlie Chaplin required 40 policemen to escort him through his fans into the hotel in 1921, Nöel Coward wrote songs at The Ritz and Tallulah Bankhead sipped Champagne from her slipper during a press conference.

The Palm Court

At the heart of The Ritz lies The Palm Court, an elegant salon originally designed as a destination for glamorous guests from high society to 'see and be seen'.

Originally known as the Winter Garden, The Palm Court is a dramatic room of fanciful design, flanked by high walls of gleaming mirrors and a ceiling seemingly woven together with intricate gilded trellis. Romantic birdcage chandeliers are adorned with ornate metal flowers, and at the centre of the room is a soaring, vibrant floral display.

The Rivoli Bar

Likened to a 'gorgeous little jewel box', The Rivoli Bar is an intimate cocktail lounge. It is overtly Art Deco in its design: a sophisticated symphony of camphor wood walls inset with illuminated Lalique glass panels, patterned mirrors, decorative bas relief, and an under-lit bar topped with polished cocktail shakers, all overarched with brilliant gilded ceiling domes.

Thistle Marble Arch

Bryanston Street, London W1H 7EH 0871 376 9027 www.thearchlondon.com

This Classic Art Deco structured hotel with its colourful circular glass ceiling decoration which greets you in the Lobby will immediately impress.

The hotel is located near Oxford Street in London and offers guests 692 spacious modern bedrooms, including 281 deluxe and executive rooms and suites to choose from. These do not have Art Deco features but the clean cut interior decoration is as pleasing.

You can enjoy cocktails served in the Glenn Miller lounge bar, or afternoon tea in the Delicacy coffee bar and dinner at the Marmor grill restaurant; are all to be savoured.

Again the surroundings are in the Modern Style, all clean cut geometric lines, with circular detail echoed in chair back or tables.

The Thistle Marble Arch hotel takes its name from one of London's best-known landmarks. Originally built on the Mall as a new gateway to Buckingham Palace, the Arch remains an exclusive thoroughfare as only members of the royal family and the King's Troop, Royal Horse Artillery, are allowed to pass through it.

As the name implies, the Arch is made from Italian white Carrara marble, a favourite material of the Art Deco movement in the 1920s and 30s, when Thistle Marble Arch was built.

Town Hall Hotel & Apartments

Patriot Square, London E2 9NF
020 7871 0460 www.townhallhotel.com

This is an upscale, chic hotel in a former Edwardian town hall with original period and art deco features. Set in the heart of the vibrant East End, Town Hall Hotel combines architectural splendour with cutting-edge design. Pevsener, the Architectural Bible of Britain, called the internal decoration 'subtle but expensive Deco style'.

Australian walnut wood was used to panel the Council Chamber, mahogany in the mayoral office, green and white marble lined the staircase, while even the air vents were covered with exquisitely patterned brass grilles. Town Hall Hotel successfully marries Edwardian, Art-Deco and cutting-edge modern architecture.

Using techniques never before seen in Britain, including a patterned metal veil, laser-cut with a design inspired by the Art-deco Council Chamber, every room is flooded with natural light, while original features have been painstakingly restored. Architects, furniture designers, artists and craftsmen have been involved at every step of the way to create a truly stunning interior.

The Montfort Suite

Soaring triple-height ceilings stretch high above, while light floods through huge arched windows, splashed with colour from stained-glass panels. At one end of the suite, stand two plaster statues made by the famous sculptor, Henry Poole: Truth holds a mirror, while Happiness carries a comic mask and wine cup.

Town Hall Hotel's unique spaces provide an inspirational setting for filming and photographic shoots. It has been featured in many films and dramas. Recent productions include 'Atonement'.

The Park Lane Hotel

Piccadilly, London W1J 7BX
020 7499 6321 Designer Kenneth Anns Architect Henry Tanner.

This hotel was opened in 1927 at the height of Art Deco's heyday, as can be clearly seen from its stylish public areas. These include its famous Ballroom which has gilded bas-reliefs above the doors and has featured in Jeeves and Wooster. Art Deco touches are everywhere. The

mirror and side table surmounted by light fitting illuminated glass and gold metal balustrade are thrilling. It is a joy to be greeted by the impressive mural in the lobby. Whether this is an informal lunch or a sumptuous Afternoon Tea, the lounge at The Palm Court is an ideal place to relax for guests and locals alike, thanks to its beautiful Art Deco surroundings and natural daylight. The Palm Court numerous awards and accolades for its English Afternoon Tea.

The Palm Court Bar

Enjoy a cocktail, a hot drink or a light snack from the extensive bar menu in The Palm Court. Fanc
soaking up the atmosphere of this traditional Art Deco gathering place while getting some wor
done? Complimentary WiFi internet access is available throughout the bar and lounge area. Som
of the Executive Rooms and all suites at The Park Lane Hotel feature authentic marble bathroom
If you stay there, you should ask for a room with views over magnificent Green Park.

Hotel 41

41 Buckingham Palace Road, London SW1W 0PP 0800 411 805

This intimate hotel comprises 28 rooms, and is a great hideaway in the busy City. The them
throughout is ebony & ivory. The immaculate furnished rooms and public areas are styled in blac
and white tiles and furnishings. It complements the dark mahogany woodwork panelling and give
that overall impression of simplistic, yet elegant, Art Deco styling.

The Waldorf Hilton Hotel

Aldwych, London WC2B 4DD 020 7836 2400

This Hotel is in the restored Edwardian Style so it will transport you back to this amazing period in time. The Art Deco features and 1930s feeling lies within the Good Godrey's Bar and Lounge and the beautiful columned swimming pool. You can select from a range of contemporary guest rooms or upgrade to a Guest Room Plus and enjoy the restored Edwardian styling.

Good Godfrey's Bar and Lounge

Good Godfrey's Bar proudly takes its name from the former leader of the Waldorf House band, the handsome and talented Howard Godfrey.

Howard Godfrey and the Waldorfians enjoyed huge success in the early 1920s as serious players in the London Social scene, boasting hit records and popular acclaim: the Best Show in Town.

Homage Restaurant

Inspired by the grand cafés of Europe, this fashionable London restaurant at The Waldorf Hilton hotel has Louis XVI-style decor. You can enjoy a glass of champagne among the chandeliers, elegant columns, leather banquets and modern art.

Imperial Hotel

61-66 Russell Square, London WC1B 5BB 020 7837 3655

The Imperial Hotel was originally opened in 1837. The reason it has been included is the wonderfu
Atrium Bar & Cafe. This amazing space with its high ceiling and island placed bar is contemporar
styled from the Art Deco period. I particularly like the interior design of the carpet and layout. The
spacious reception foyer harks back to another era with light wooden panelling and impressive
lightshades. The bedrooms are of a light and airy contemporary design.

LONDON RESTAURANTS, BARS & CAFES

The restaurants, cafes and bars that are included are either independent or incorporated in one of the hotel chains, many of which are detailed in the London Accommodation section. As previously stated, the fabulous bars, restaurants and foyers in the Grand Hotels are open to non-residents, so you can savour the Art Deco features without staying the night, if that suits your plans and budget better.

Dinner and Afternoon Tea reservations do need to be booked in advance to assure availability, but you may be lucky and get a cancellation on the day as long as you are flexible and have a back-up plan.

Some of the bars that are listed, are described as 'Speakeasies'. These originally were the places for illegal boozing that came to prominence during the Prohibition era in 1920s America. Since then, they have taken on a mythical status. Just think of overflowing gin glasses, sassy and suave jazz musicians, and a glitzy dress code.

The following bars are included because they capture this time in history, of the late 1920s and 30s, but are not necessarily Art Deco in architectural design.

Bibendum Restaurant

Michelin House, 81 Fulham Road, London SW3 6RD Tel 020 7581 5817

This amazing building was commissioned by the Michelin Tyre Co. as their first permanent British Headquarters in 1909, and is an iconic landmark. In 1985 Michelin moved out of the building and in June of that year it was bought by Sir Terence Conran and Paul Hamlyn.

Dining at the Restaurant is a visual feast, as well as a treat for the taste buds. During the day, light

streams through the spectacular stained glass windows. The high ceilinged Restaurant buzzes with activity. It is the sense of elegance and glamour that always make it feel like a special occasion when dining here.

The individual style of the building and interior has been described as an example of Art Nouveau, Proto-Art Deco, and geometrical Classicism. Designed by an employee of the company, under the guidance of Edouard and Andre Michelin, the imagination and vivacity created an architectural statement of its time.

Brasserie Zedel

20 Sherwood Street, Soho, London W1F 7ED 020 7734 4888

Every building tells a story, and on first glance you could easily walk past this without sampling its hidden delights. It is well worth absorbing the history behind this sublime Brasserie, as when you arrive and descend the stairs the surroundings engulf your senses and you became so excited that it is difficult to fully appreciate this building.

Brasserie Zedel was once part of The Regent Palace Hotel, which was built by 'T Lyons & Co. Ltd' and opened in 1915. It was designed in the Beaux Arts style and was the largest hotel in Europe at the time, with 1,028 bedrooms.

The early part of the 1930s, the English architect Oliver Bernard OBE (1881-1939) who was also a scenic, graphic and industrial designer, was commissioned to redesign the interiors. Bernard was recognised as a key figure in the creation of the Art Deco style. He was the technical director of the British Pavilion at the Paris 1925 Art Deco Exhibition (Exposition Internationale des Arts decoratifs et Industriels Modernes).

He was commissioned to work as consultant on various other projects, including J. Lyons & Co designing the interiors of their Oxford Street, Coventry Street, and Strand Corner Houses. In

1929 he created the spectacular Art Deco entrance to the Strand Palace Hotel.

After the Second World War, like many grand establishments, Zedel gradually declined. Then in 2004, renowned Dixon Jones architects worked with Donald Insall Associates to restore it to it former glory days in the 1930s Art Deco style.

he Crazy Coqs Caberet & Bar has been immaculately recreated from the original 1934 architectural drawings. The hallway of tobacco coloured travertine is retained in the foyer, and the Bar Americain has impressive broad, horizontal stripes of stained birch veneers and jazz age columns.

The inexpensive French cuisine, in the divine surroundings, a definite for your wish list. I can assure you that you will not be disappointed.

Oxo Tower Restaurant

8th Floor Oxo Tower Wharf, Bargehouse Street, South Bank, London SE1 9PH
020 7803 388 oxo.reservations@harveynichols.com

The rooftop Oxo Tower Restaurant, Brasserie, and Bar opened in 1996. Situated in this iconic Art Deco building, it has stunning views across London. The ultra-modern interior features a unique ceiling with blue neon lights, which creates the atmosphere of a beautiful moonlit night. The leather clad bars and slate tables fit in well with the 'moderne' new look. There is an innovative cocktail list, and they have live jazz sessions on certain days.

The Wolseley Restaurant

160 Piccadilly, London W1J 9ED 020 7499 6996

The Wolseley Restaurant is situated next to the Ritz Hotel, so you cannot miss it and should not miss it. This beautiful building was originally constructed in 1921 as a car showroom for Wolseley Motors. It only served this purpose for six year until 1927 when Barclay's Bank took it over and traded from the building until 1999. After extensive renovation it opened as a restaurant in 2003. It has glorious Art Deco features of polished Portland stone and the floor is black and white marble in geometric designs. The Doric columns and elaborate bronze pendant lighting and concealed lamps reflect light into the domes. It is such an occasion to enjoy breakfast or Afternoon tea in this incredible building.

Oscar Restaurant at Charlotte Street Hotel

5-17 Charlotte Street, London WIT IRJ 020 7980 1007

This is a modern contemporary designed restaurant, which has a decisive Art Deco feel to it. It has large colourful decorated murals to the walls and furnishings with real pizzazz.

The following are within the **Dorchester Hotel**

Bar 45 As well as serving a varied selection of unique cocktails, Bar 45 boasts the largest selection of American wines in the United Kingdom. A bar menu of 'Rough cuts' by Wolfgang Puck includes Mini Wagyu Sliders, Dorset Crab and Lobster "Louis" Rolls. Sumptuous surroundings and a contemporary design make this a memorable experience.

The Grill First established in 1931, The Grill at the Dorchester quickly gained a reputation as the place to be for some of the finest grill food in London. The restaurant features a striking, hand-blown Murano glass chandelier and contrasting natural materials including zinc, copper and marble, set against butterscotch leather and oak parquet flooring. Pivoting wall panels create a separate ambience from day to night, creating an inviting atmosphere morning to night.

Cut Cut restaurant has striking Art Deco influences which are juxtaposed with cutting edge contemporary art. With its vibrant interiors and enticing menu, created by internationally acclaimed chef founder Wolfgang Puck, CUT is a modern American steak restaurant. On Sundays, relax with brunch and a Bloody Mary, custom-made to your liking, as you listen to live music.

China Tang Conceived by Sir David Tang, the founder of China Clubs in Hong Kong, Peking and Singapore, this restaurant offers some of the best and most authentic Cantonese food outside China. The sumptuous interior, which is designed to evoke a romantic sense of the art deco of the Thirties, with an abundance of chinoiserie and quirky objets d'art, showcases a collection of both traditional and contemporary Chinese art, with 1930s Jazz every Tuesday. It also has 3 private dining rooms aptly named Ping, Pang and Pong.

The Promenade Guests entering The Dorchester are greeted with the stunning vista of The Promenade, which stretches the same length as the London landmark, Nelson's Column.

efurbished in 2005 by Thierry Despont, The Promenade is a series of rich, warm, intimate spaces ulminating in a stunning, oval leather bar at the end of the room. Very much the heart of the hotel, he Promenade is open all day for informal dining, serving breakfast, morning coffee, lunch, ternoon tea and a supper menu. It features live entertainment on a daily basis. A pianist plays om 1:15pm to 7:00pm and live jazz music plays from 7:30pm each day.

___

he *following are within the* **Savoy Hotel**

avoy Grill This is one of London's most legendary restaurants which was frequented by celebrated ners such as Sir Winston Churchill, Oscar Wilde, Frank Sinatra and HM Queen Elizabeth, The ueen Mother. The original seating plan has been brought back for its reopening.

esigner Russell Sage took inspiration from the restaurant's heyday, and original 1920's Art Deco atures have been restored.

uests can also enjoy classic cocktails in Knight's Bar, an art deco cocktail lounge located on the st floor. It is the perfect place to enjoy either a pre-dinner cocktail or after-dinner aperitif.

merican Bar The term 'American Bar' refers to a bar serving mixed or 'American' style drinks, ore commonly known as cocktails. As transatlantic travel became more popular in the late 19th

and early 20th Centuries, many American Bars opened throughout London. The American Bar The Savoy is the longest surviving of these.

In 1903 the first truly 'famous' bartender arrived at The American Bar, a lady named Ada 'Cole Coleman, who's signature cocktail was the Hanky Panky, still a popular choice today. Ada's success was the inspirational Harry Craddock, who not only created a number of classic cocktails but wh notoriously compiled these recipes into the legendary Savoy Cocktail book, still regarded today the bartender's bible.

Kaspars Bar & Grill Kaspar's offers an informal yet luxury all-day dining experience in an elega 1920s style. Specialises in, fresh seafood and the finest artisan cheeses.

Beaufort Bar The Beaufort Bar provides a theatrical, art deco setting in which to enjoy cockta that push the boundaries. The bar itself stands on the hotel's former cabaret stage, which w graced by such luminaries as Carol Gibbons, the Savoy Orpheans and George Gershwin.

A tradition of live entertainment continues to this day with nightly performances by both renowne and up and coming talent, as well as monthly evenings of Cabaret and Burlesque.

Thames Foyer The Thames Foyer is very much the heart of The Savoy. A stunning glass dome floods this sociable spot with wonderful natural light – and beneath this, a pianist serenades guests from a winter garden gazebo, as they enjoy the world-famous afternoon tea.

Situated within **Claridge's Hotel**

Vera at Claridge's This Michelin starred restaurant has a creative and natural take on modern British Cuisine. The name derives from the Latin word for 'wild', which reflects the ethos of the restaurant. The surroundings are impeccable, being original Art Deco from floor to ceiling.

The following are within the **Wellesley Hotel**

The Crystal Bar This lavish Bar with authentic 1920's furniture and decorative features is heaven. Whilst sipping a cocktail you can hear the music from the Jazz Lounge.

The Oval This intimate restaurant as the name suggests is aesthetically very pleasing in the oval shape arranged like a stage setting. The stylish seating arrangement of furnishings creates contemporary atmosphere. It has space for 28 dinners and specialises in Italian cuisine.

The following are within the **Beaumont Hotel**

The Colony Grill Room The Colony takes its lead from the traditional Grill Rooms original found in London and New York, and serves appropriately classic dishes from both sides of the Atlantic. I particularly like the interior design of 1930s images which adorn the walls.

American Bar This bar is affectionately know as 'Jimmy's', and during the 1920s and early 1930s these type of bars were prevalent in London and Paris. It specialises in Bourbons and American Whiskies. Cocktails are strictly only shaken or stirred they state nothing new fangled here! It certainly gives you that feel that Hemingway and Fitzgerald would have felt at home here.

Situated within the **Park Lane Hotel**

The Palm Court Bar and Lounge incorporating Bracewells The Palm Court is one of London's most prestigious Art Deco landmarks. The original features date back to 1927. It has a marble floor, the original bar and a high curved ceiling. Enjoying afternoon tea, while listening to the relaxing resident harpist takes you back to the prosperity of the late 1920s London.

The most hospitable staff will oblige you by showing you the glorious ballroom and if possible give you a mini tour of the other outstanding features.

Situated within **The Ritz**

The Rivoli Bar The Rivoli Bar is an intimate cocktail lounge which is overtly Art Deco in its desig a sophisticated symphony of camphor wood walls inset with illuminated Lalique glass panel patterned mirrors, decorative bas relief, and an under-lit bar topped with polished cocktail shaker all overarched with brilliant gilded ceiling domes. This has the right balance of sophistication an opulence.

he Palm Court The Palm Court is not Art Deco, so please allow me to add this outstanding enue on the merit that it does epitomise the whole late 20s – 30s fun loving, decadent, and utrageously opulent era. Originally known as the Winter Garden, The Palm Court is a dramatic oom of fanciful design, flanked by high walls of gleaming mirrors, a ceiling seemingly woven together ith intricate gilded trellis, romantic birdcage chandeliers adorned with ornate metal flowers, a riking stone fountain inhabited by large gilded statues and at the centre of the room a soaring, brant floral display. When sampling the delicious food it is difficult to take yours eyes away from e elaborate surroundings, but then you don't need to. Just sit and soak up the exuberant mosphere.

tuated within the **Warldorf Hotel**

ood Godfrey's Bar and Lounge Contemporary style bar which again could have come out of e 1930s. The signature cocktails include The Astor Hip Flask, named after William Waldorf Astor. he refined Madam cocktail was inspired by the soubriquet of 'Madam Geneva' for the badly made n available during the gin craze of Georgian London.

Bob Bob Ricard

1 Upper James Street, Soho,
London W1F 9DF

When you arrive at this Restaurant the
name does not belie the Faberge Egg
feast for your eyes that awaits. You
enter a world of mirrors, marble,
polished brass, and theatrical velvet
drapes.   Art Deco   motifs   and
chandeliers adorn the ceilings and
walls. The late David Collins (who
designed other top restaurants The Ivy
and The Wolseley) is responsible for
the opulent and decadent interior.

The boothed restaurant on the ground floor is uniform in royal blue, whilst in the basement Club
Room, red is the *de rigueur*, it does not scream out ostentation as the soft lighting and furnishing
make it tasteful and decadent. Each booth has its own 'Press for Champagne' button should your
bottle or glass run dry, but the pink waist-coated staff who are unobtrusive but very attentive a
never far away. After eating here you really do feel that you have stepped out of a 1930s Hollywood
movie.

Quaglino's

16 Bury Street, London SW1Y 6AJ 020 7930 6767 quaglinos@danddlondon.com

Quaglino's is not only a stylish restaurant but doubles as an all round entertainment venue. It has two bars, the original, iconic main balcony bar and a new show stopping circular bar, which is called The Q Bar, positioned right at the heart of the restaurant. This venue has a rich 1930s heritage and cabaret acts and talented musicians perform most evenings from 10pm. Once inside this marvellous decadent palace the overall feeling is that of the 1930s sassy jazz age. It has the added bonus that no charge is levied to enter, so you can enjoy the entertainment for free, whilst sipping a delicious drink with a great view from The Q Bar.

Fischer's Restaurant

50 Marylebone High Street, London W1U 5HN 020 7466 5501 info@fischers.co.uk

This restaurant offers a classic Viennese menu from breakfast to full evening dinner service. This includes an extensive choice of cured fish, salads, schnitzels, sausages, and sandwiches along with an impressive vegetarian menu. The delicious strudels, biscuits and ice-cream coupes are not to be missed. It has an amazing decorative interior.

(Photos ©corbinandking.com)

Boulestin Restaurant & Café Marcel

5 St James's Street, London SW1A 1EP 020 7930 2030

The beautiful clean and classic Deco interior of Boulestin is all about classic French food. This restaurant and café was inspired by Xavier Marcel Boulestin, renowed food expert, writer and the proprietor of the original restaurant which opened in 1927.

More than half of the dishes on the menu are from Boulestin's pre-war cookbook including Oeuf en Gelee, Jambon Persille, and Cassoulet. Café Marcel is the perfect spot to escape to.

Donald Moffat wrote in The New Yorker in 1932 that Xavier Marcel Boulestin is *"Doctor of the Philosophy of the table, Culinary Ambassador to the English, intelligent gentleman of France, man of the world, essayist of vigour and charm…"*

Berners Tavern in the London Edition Hotel

) Berners Street, London WLT 3LF 020 7908 7979

ocated in Fitzrovia on the edge of London's Soho neighbourhood, this luxury boutique hotel reserves the finest aspects of an iconic landmark building, but reinvents the spaces within to create dynamic fusion of old and new, past and present. Hence the Berners Tavern in this restored dwardian building, with grandeur to rival most, will thrill you.

has a relaxing taupe and rose palette with an impressive art display featuring over 300 pictures. he grand ceiling light, curved seating areas and dining tables are evocative of an Art Deco time.

Corinthia Hotel

Vhithall Place, London SW1A 2BD 020 7930 8181 London@corinthia.com

Massimo Restaurant and Oyster Bar

he Northall Bar, featuring a marble island, is the epitome of chic in London. You can p an aperitif or classic cocktail and it offers a all-day light lunch and dinner menu for e casual diner.

assimo Restaurant was designed by David ollins Studio. The art deco style brings gether statuesque Corinthian columns ning the dining room, hovering globe light tings, sleek mahogany, and glossy marble. he striking surroundings can only mpliment the delicious Italian food.

assoon Bar combines a relaxed and intimate ambience with a stimulating dash of theatre. Your ocktail, spirit or champagne is served in elegant replicas of Queen Victoria's glassware. The seven etre bar appears to sweep seamlessly into the Roland piano. Jazz inspired art from William H hnson and an Art Deco design signature the spirit and rhythm of the 1920s music room makes r a luxurious den.

The following are within the **Hotel Café Royal**
68 Regent Street, London W1B 4DYT 020 7406 3310

The Café Created from golden Sienna marble, The Café is a beautiful, calming space fronti
London's vibrant Regent Street. Celebrating the European tradition of café culture, The Café offe
a light menu of seasonal dishes alongside an espresso bar and counters lined with cakes, pastri
and chocolates in the most decadent surroundings.

Green Bar Inspired by the Café Royal Cocktail Book compiled in 1937, the Green Bar is a vibra
cocktail destination for contemporary Londoners and hotel guests. Celebrating the diverse histo
of the location, the cocktail list features heritage cocktails alongside classic concoctions and
selection of small dining plates.

The Absinthe Journey' is an iconic offering from the Green Bar. Expert bartenders mix cocktails and serve shots straight up traditionally, from the steady drizzle of the Absinthe fountain. As the spirit of Café Royal is revived, so too is the ritual of drinking Absinthe, the favoured tipple of the Bohemian intellects, who were famous or infamous for notoriously frequenting Café Royal throughout its history, creating a colourful and decadent past.

Ten Room The Ten Room offers British informal dining all-day in the heart of Hotel Café Royal in the centre of London's West End. The revival of the Ten Room signals the resurgence of one of London's most renowned dining rooms. Echoing the heritage of this iconic landmark, this elegant space has been both sensitively restored to feature original details and modernised to appeal to twenty-first century sensibilities.

The Ten Room is open from 7am to 10.30pm. Breakfast, lunch, cream tea, pre and post theatre dinner are served, as well as an additional menu that features an edited selection of favourites available throughout the day and into late evening.

O.W.B Short for the Oscar Wilde Bar, formerly the iconic Grill Room, this bar has been exquisitely restored to its authentic Louis XVI detailing. Not Art Deco in style but those 'bright young things' of the 1920s/30s era certainly frequented this place to enjoy champagne and lap up the outstanding glamour and atmosphere.

The Black Cat Cabaret Presented by The Black Cat Cabaret, 'Salon des Artistes' is a decadent display within the finely gilded and mirrored splendour of the Oscar Wilde Bar. Cabaret singers, character comedians, highly-skilled performance artistes, magicians and live musicians perform a captivating show. You can enjoy the show alone or chose to dine first. That feeling of Isherwood's 'Cabaret' and the delicious 'melting pot' of 1930s entertainment is perfectly relived.

The Domino The Domino is the new, refined dining experience completing Hotel Café Royal' return to London's vibrant social scene. Revivifying the glamour of entertaining, members of Th Club at Café Royal and hotel guests will dine under an elegant canopy of intricate and beautiful restored cartouches, like the icons of London society before them.

The Delaunay

55 Aldwych, London WC2B 4BB 020 7499 8558

With a delightful Viennese-inspired menu th Delaunay Restaurant has Art Deco leanings in th design and interior decoration and is just wonderf to sit and relax in, whatever the time of day.

If you don't want to sit in the main restaurant Th Counter at Delaunay, with a separate entrance c Aldwych has a similar menu. I particularly like th décor here as it conjures up the flavour of tha period of time in Vienna.

The blue and white tiled walls and internal fixtur and fittings are all Art Deco sourced and inspired

Sketch

9 Conduit Street, London W1S 2XG 020 7659 4500

Ascend the stairs to the Lecture Room & Library, Sketch's two Michelin starred fine dini restaurants, and enjoy the spectacle to follow. Created by leading interior designer Gahba O'Keeffe, in an eclectic Art Deco style, all 'singing and dancing' glorious carpet and décor ju enhances the 'tasting' and 'a la carte' menus devised by French Master Chef Pierre Gagnaire.

Kettner's Bar

9 Romily Street, Soho, London WID 5HP 020 7734 6112

The building was originally a series of four Georgian town houses, and in 1867 August Kettner chef to Napoleon III) opened it as a restaurant. It soon became infamous as the rendezvous for eliciously colourful characters of the time. Oscar Wilde was a regular and mentions this in his ial notes. Agatha Christie and Bing Crosby were also celebrated patrons. King Edward VII

conducted his affair with Lillie Langtry here and even ordered a secret tunnel to be built between ettner's and the Palace Theatre where she performed on stage. Apparently they used the tunnel o meet at Kettner's during the intervals. The glamorous interior has deco touches in the light ttings and bar area, but look out for the celebrated 1920s /30s evenings which only add to the hole experience.

Patisserie Valerie

4 Old Compton St, Soho, London WID 4TY 020 7437 3466 www.patisserie-valerie.co.uk

atisserie Valerie was first opened in Frith Street in London's Soho in 1926 by Belgian born Madam alerie. She came to London on a mission to introduce fine Continental Patisserie to the English. was an instant success. Now in London there are thirty Patisserie Valerie cafes dotted all over, om Belgravia to Wimbledon. Inside they are all kept in the deco style to varying degrees, with eating, lighting and wide glassed counters. Please see their website for all the listings in London.

E Pellicci Cafe

32 Bethnal Green Road, London E2 OAG 020 7739 4873

It is well worth the fifteen minute walk from Liverpool Street Station to this family owned premises. Upon entering you are instantly thrown back to another century. The warm wooden marquetry interior which was crafted by Achille Capocci in 1946 (each panel being crafted separately when the then proprietor could afford it), is a thing of classic beauty in the Art Deco style. The hospitality and food are second to none. It offers full English Breakfast with Italian Cuisine and has a surprisingly good vegetarian option, I can vouch for Mama Pellicci's bread pudding.

Le QuecumBar & Brasserie

42-44 Battersea High Street, London SW11 3HX 020 7787 2227

The Parisian 1930s cafe-society setting is a perfect backdrop for the earthy ambience of Le Quecum Bar. The collaboration between hot gypsy swing created by the Gypsy guitar master Django Reinhardt in the hot club era of Paris in the 1930s blends seamlessly with the jazz music. You can soak up the nightly live music, enjoy delicate French cuisine and sample fine (as well as inexpensive) world wines - all in this sizzling yet laid back club on Battersea High Street.

The Nightjar

129 City Road, London EC1V 1JB 020 7253 4101

Its basement location and stunning vintage décor give Nightjar all the authentic glamour of the 1920s speakeasy. With prohibition-themed cocktails and vintage spirits, this subterranean bar with live jazz and swing music will certainly get your feet tapping.

Floridita

00 Wardour Street, London W1F 0TN
20 7314 4000

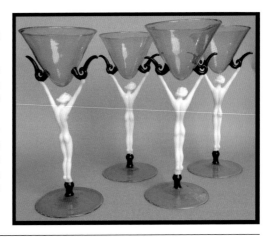

Based on the world famous El Floridita in Havana, this Soho bar emulates 1930s Cuba by serving up Latin American style food and an extensive cocktail menu.

For cigar lovers, it also has it own cigar menu and humidor. A live music programme including authentic Cuban bands enhances the traditional Latin atmosphere; it's a fantastic venue to dance the night away.

xperimental Cocktail Club

3A Gerrard Street Chinatown, London W1D 5PS
20 7434 3559 reservation@chinatownecc.com

This Cocktail Club in a speakeasy-style basement is hidden behind a Chinatown door. It is meant o be hard to find, which just adds to the mystique. Inside remains opulent and elegantly aloof to different trends arranged over 3 floors. It is best to make an email reservation: they do keep space or walk in guests but it is a first come first served basis.

Colbert

0-52 Sloane Square, Chelsea SW1W 8AX www.colbertchelsea.com 020 7730 2804

ou cannot help but be spellbound by this café which is inspired by the great boulevard cafés of aris, Colbert sits where Chelsea, Knightsbridge & Belgravia meet next to The Royal Court Theatre. he premises have slowly expanded over the last nine decades from one room to three to cater or its ever increasing clientele. It has an interesting collection of art and local memorabilia inside nd has the true spirit of traditional French Cafes from the 1920s and 30s. It is open 7 days a veek, from breakfast until late.

Les Deux Salons

40-42 William IV Street, London WC2N 4DD
020 7420 2050 www.lesdeuxsalons.co.uk Designer Terance Conran

This duo of new high-end bistro and restaurant is a testament to the talent of designer Teranc
Conran. He has created an authentic French Brasserie which transports you back to the opuler
and sophisticated 1920s and 30s with furnishings and fittings. The ground floor is the buzzing bistr
area and any moment I half expected to see Toulouse Lautrec or Josephine Baker grace th
establishment. Upstairs is the fine dining restaurant, more intimate but just as beautiful. It is
fabulous venue for a pre or post supper when visiting theatre land.

LONDON THEATRES & CINEMAS

Theatres

London's theatres have a long history dating back to the 1500s when William Shakespeare was famously creating his name as a masterful playwright and actor. Those theatres, which thrived back then have disappeared; the majority of theatres we see today were built during the reign of Queen Victoria (1845-1901), with some during the Edwardian time (1901-1910). Only a few theatres that were built during the 1920s and 30s incorporated Art Deco, either in the exterior architecture or internal fittings and décor. Unlike the cinemas which were having their heyday during this period, the theatres, now having a rival, did not have the impetus or funds to refurbish in the new 'moderne' style, they stayed with the tried and tested traditional décor, which we can still abundantly see today, in all its glory.

Prince Edward Theatre

Old Compton Street, London W1D 4HS 0844 482 5151
1930 Designed by Edward A Stone Built by Griggs & Son

This theatre opened to the comedy musical Rio Rita by Harry Tierney on the 3rd April 1930. Its subtle art deco auditorium and interior, designed by Marc-Henri Levy and Gaston Laverdet, is decorated in shades of fuchsia and gold. It is opulent and decadent but with taste. Just like the tantalising Josephine Baker, who even debuted her famous 'Banana Dance' here, with a four week season in 1933, where she was billed as 'The Idol of Europe'.

Over the years it has been a casino and cinema, but each time it has been sympathetically remodelled and refurbished, not losing its original Art Deco features in the foyer and the main auditorium.

Apollo Victoria Theatre

17 Wilton Road, Westminster, London SW1V 1LG
0844 871 3001 1929 Architect Earnest Walmsley Lewis

This most impressive art deco styled theatre was built mainly from concrete and was originall
opened as a state-of-the-art cinema, to accommodate the growing popularity of the 'talkies'. Th
spectacular nautical theme inside features columns with fountains and shells that appear to flov
from within. At the time the Gaumont British News called the theatre 'a fairy cavern under th
sea, or a mermaid's dream of heaven'.

Adelphi Theatre

409-412 The Strand, London WC2R ONS
020 3725 7060 1930 Architect Earnest Schaufelberg

This Theatre is very modern looking with a black minimalist art deco façade which has an octagona
geometric design. The look is retained in some of the lobby fittings such as the booking window
which still have the classic art deco script.

Prince of Wales Theatre

Coventry Street, London W1D 6AS
0844 482 5115 1884 (Rebuilt 1937) Robert Cromie Architect C.J. Phipps

The Prince of Wales sits proudly on the corner of Coventry Street. The exterior Deco tower
brightly lit and a wonderful collection of framed playbills and programmes, along with deco mirror
and sculptures, greet you in the foyer.

During 1927, Agatha Christies 'The Blue Train' was performed with Charles Laughton as Hercule Poiro
In 1930 the then, new manager Edith Evans, starred in Delilah, but this was not a success so the theatr
looked for alternative shows to bring in the money. They decided to show the risqué 'Folies' sty
revues, which included Voila! Les Dames, which proved to be such a success that they funded th
rebuilding of the theatre in 1937.

Cinemas

Following the horrors of the First World War, cinemas were welcomed with opened arms. The escapism, affordable glamour and wonderment at the new technology available to all, captivated the public in their millions.

With cinemas, unlike designs for commercial or residential properties, the architects were unencumbered by the irritant of windows: they were able to create majestic viewing halls in virtually any shape that could be imagined and engineered. They were encouraged to add as much glamour, spectacle, scale, and exoticism that could be incorporated. Fortunately for us, some of this can still be seen today.

In Central and Greater London alone there are over eighty cinemas listed by the Cinema Theatre Association, each with its own unique story to tell. I have listed the venues that I feel most reflect the Art Deco period in time, either physically incorporating the exterior architectural design and/or interiorly creating the Art Deco period by interior design and furnishings.

The Grand Odeon Cinemas

Sadly, many have been demolished, and many are now occupied by other premises, but there are still some glorious cinemas out there to visit.

The founder of the Odeon chain, Oscar Deutsch was at the helm of a new cutting edge design. He decided to part with the traditional style and interior decoration of theatres and embrace sharp and striking facades with neon light and strong vertical and horizontal lines. Inside he created a showbiz of glitz and glamour with the foyers, incorporating sleek curves and glittering lighting which transfixed the theatregoers. By 1939 he had 136 Odeon's to his name, all in this style. Oscar Deutsch employed Harry Weedon an English architect, to oversee the Art Deco designs of his cinemas during the 1930s. He was prolific architect throughout his life, but will always be best know for his role in the groundbreaking Odeon Cinemas.

Odeon have 26 cinemas in London including 5 IMAX cinemas showing the latest 3D films. Listed below are the Odeons' which still retain much of their original Art Deco features either in the exterior architecture and/or the interior. Odeon has adapted over the years, but still retained and remained loyal to the original style with Deco touches, even in the impressive state of the art new IMAX cinemas.

The Odeon Leicester Square

24-26 Leicester Square, London WC2H 7LQ 0871 224 4007

This cinema you cannot miss, for the sheer scale of the huge black polished granite façade which has a tower standing at 120 feet high displaying in neon lights the name. This architectural design is Streamline Moderne as adopted by Oscar Deutsch for his empire of cinemas.

Odeon Cinema Muswell Hill

Fortis Road, Muswell Hill, London N10 3HP 1936 Designed by George Coles

This Cinema is the epitome of 1930s art deco style, and is a Grade II listed property. The cinema was converted in standard style to a triple in the 1970s. A wall was dropped from the circle and the stalls divided into 2 cinemas. It is screen 1 which displays art deco at its finest. Along the ceiling and leading to the screen is a stylish motif, resembling a strip of film. Either side of the screen are the iconic Odeon clocks. The foyer and all internal parts are otherwise much the same as they would have been on opening. The exterior has the typical faiencing. Thoughtfully, in the design stage, the entrance was changed to face Fortis Green Road, to avoid offending the sensibilities of the congregation of the local church.

All the following Odeon Cinemas have Art Deco features. Please see the website www.odeon.co.uk t[
view them online and to book tickets.

Camden
14 The Parkway
Camden
NW1 7AA

Barnet
Great North Road
Barnet
EN5 1AB

Beckenham
The High Street
Beckenham
BR3 1DY

Holloway
419-427 Holloway Road
Holloway
N7 6LJ

Kensington
High Street
W8 6NA

Richmond
72 Hill Street
Richmond
TW9 1RW

South Woodford
60-64 High Road
Woodford
E18 2QL

Swiss Cottage
96 Finchley Road
NW3 5EL

Wimbledon
39 The Broadway
SW19 1QB

Everyman Cinemas

It appears that Everyman Cinemas are all about that little extra when you go to view the lates[
release. They are a new take on the old style and glamour that you would expect when going ou[
for the evening. Expect comfort, and cosyness in delightful surroundings. Some of them have mor[
Art Deco features than others, with the interior and furnishing more to this period in time. Other[
are more a window to the past when going to the cinema was a very special occasion.

Everyman Belize Park

203 Haverstock Hill, Belsize Park NW3 4QG 0871 906 9060

This intimate cinema has a stage at the front of the auditorium with a reception area and bar. [
has 16 premier luxury leather seats with reclining backrests and footrests, with 113 standard seat[
and leather armchairs and sofas. The total capacity is 129.

Everyman Canary Wharf

Crossrail Place, Level 2, Canary Wharf E14 5AR 0871 906 9060

This cinema has three different screens; Screen 1 with a seating capacity of 109, screen 2 – 52 an[
screen 3 – 105. They all have a mixture of premier armchair and sofa seating with footrests (som[
of the armchairs are Art Deco in style, as is the interior wall decoration).

Everyman Hampstead

5 Holly Bush Vale, Hampstead NW3 6TX 0871 906 9060

This cinema has two screens and an upper lounge for private screening which seats 15 adults c[
17 children. Screen one has a capacity for 122 and has 82 unique armchairs and sofas, along with [
two-seater deluxe sofas and 24 leather armchairs in the private screening Gallery.

Everyman Maida Vale

215 Sutherland Avenue, Maida Vale W9 1RU 0871 906 9060

This cinema has two screens. The larger screen seats 107 with sofas and armchairs. The sma[
screen two has a capacity for 41, again with the comfy seating.

Everyman Screen on the Green

3 Upper Street, Islington N1 0NP 0871 906 9060

his Everyman is what you would expect from all the other little gems, with the luxurious seating, nd a125 capacity. It also has a stage and bar at the back of the screen.

Everyman Walton on Thames

5-89 High Street, Walton on Thames KT12 1DN 0871 906 9060

his Everyman cinema has 2 screens, one with 90 seating capacity the other with 60. It has great atures harking back to that bygone era: the bright orange Deco style seats add that extra little it of glamour.

Troxy

90 Commercial Road, Bethnal Green E1 0HN 020 7790 9000

he Troxy originally opened as a grand cinema in 1933 and was designed to seat an audience of ,520 people. The cinema had luxurious seating areas and glamorous mirror lined restaurants. The rge foyer with sweeping staircase, chandeliers, and floor to ceiling mirrors. Thick luxurious carpets, ive the cinemagoer Hollywood glamour.

he Troxy staff all wore evening dress, and even sprayed perfume during showings to make the inema goers feel good.

During its original heyday stars such as Gracie Fields, Clarke Gable and the Andrews Sisters were osted. The first film shown was 'King Kong' Over the years it has been home to the London Royal Opera Centre, where it was used for their rehearsals.

hen it became a Mecca bingo hall, until it finally closed in 2005. The current owners are Ashburn states, who have restored the venue as much possible to its original glory, whilst incorporating he needs of today's event requirements. It really does have the best of both worlds.

Vue Cinema

3 Cranbourn Street, Leicester Square WC2H 7AL
08712 240 240 1938 Architects E.A. Stone and T.R. Somerford

The Vue Cinema was originally known as the Warner Brothers Cinema. It has striking bas relief panels by Bainbridge Copanll in each corner depicting the spirits of sight and sound. With the concave façade and central tower, the simple but very effective design is well worth the visit.

The Phoenix Cinema

52 High Road N2 9PJ 020 8444 67 89 1912

Like most cinemas this is no exception to having a colourful history. It started out life in 1912 as the Picturedome, then the Coliseum in 1924-36, the Rex in 1937-75, when it was purchased by Contemporary Films, and subsequently renamed the Phoenix. In 1983 with the decline in cinema goers, property developers applied to have office blocks built. Fortunately for us it still lives to tell the tale as the proposal did not go through, due to strong opposition from local residents and the backing of the actress Maureen Lipman.

Today, the Phoenix is a non-profit making registered Trust and protected from demolition or any damaging alterations due to acquiring Grade II listing status with English Heritage in 2000. They recognised the importance of the Phoenix's original 1910 barrel vaulted ceiling and the 1938 Moll and Egan decorative wall panels. It really is a Golden age of cinema experience to visit here, the neon lighted exterior welcomes you with the glitz and glamour of the 30s and the intimate auditorium with decorative glass wall panels feels opulent and personal.

The Rio Cinema

107 Kingsland High Street, E8 2PB 020 7241 9410
1915 Architects Percy Adams, Frederick E Bromige & George Coles

This independent cinema started life as the Kingsland Empire. It was in the 1930s that it was significantly changed and it reopened as the Classic cinema in 1937 and looks much the same today as it did then. It became the Rio in 1976 and is a glorious venue with a single screen and a grand, two floor auditorium. The exterior is streamline modern with distinctive angular piles.

Watford Colosseum

Rickmansworth Road, Watford WD17 3JN
0845 075 3993 1938 Architect Charles Cowles-Voysey

Watford Colosseum started life as the Watford Town Hall Assembly Rooms and is built in the typical streamlined and cube Art Deco style used for civic buildings during this time.

The warm brick exterior has a modern contemporary feel inside, and can accommodate over 1,300 guests to live music and entertainment. It is renowned for its fine acoustic quality, which was analysed. The results found that the size and 'shoebox' shape of the hall, the flat floor, and the materials used in construction all contributed to the pleasant reverberation and sound quality of the marvellous venue.

Upon entering, The Grand Lobby Bar and Kiosk greet you and the refreshing Deco Bar which is situated in the circle is open on most show nights. The buildings newly refurbished look was completed in 2011 when it was converted into the Colosseum and is well in keeping with the exterior.

Wilton's Music Hall

Graces Alley, London E1 8JB 020 7702 2789 www.wiltons.org.uk

No, this is not art deco and you may ask why it is in this book. It dates from the mid 1800s as a music hall. Prior to this the building dates back to the 1600s, but when you enter and see the mahogany panelled bar area and the main auditorium you will realise why I had to include it. The magnificent barrel shape ceiling of the auditorium looks very modern for its time and you can see and feel the presence of all those music hall stars from over the years and especially from the 1920s and 30s.

There has been a long campaign to save this historic building which is continually in the process of renovation and refurbishment. They hold some memorable events throughout the year and the pre-booked tours which last approximately 1 hour are fascinating.

LONDON LIDOS

'A Public swimming pool that is outside or part of a beach where people can swim, lie in the sun c do water sports'

The official definition of the Lido as quoted by the Cambridge University Dictionary, appears t omit one word that sums up the Art Deco period – that of fashionable. When one hears this wor it immediately conjures up the iconic poster prints of ultra slim 'gal' in swimming hat perfectly poise ready to dive into the inviting water.

On a personal note, I cannot think of anything nicer than swimming outdoors, preferably on a war summers' day. You can have so much fun exploring the many Open Air Lidos in and around Londo on warm, hot and decidedly chilly days: the whole experience is highly exhilarating. Firstly, you ar captivated by the architecture, then the feeling of stepping into a 'time warp' and recreating tha feeling of living History. Included here are a wide selection of venues which do include natural wate areas, original Art Deco Lidos and modern open air pools which lend to the Art Deco Period. Pleas always bear in mind safety aspects when swimming outside, as the water is much colder, and yo won't need me to say that even on a warm summers' day you will need to bring plenty of war clothes for after your swim. It is always recommended to wear a swim hat, firstly to retain heat b of course to 'look the part'. You may not want to go the 'whole hog' and get your knitted swimwea out, but I do recommend putting on a Skirtini or traditional trunks to enhance the whole experienc

Please check with each venue, as to times and prices as these will obviously vary from season t season. Even if you do not want to take the plunge, it is well worth the ticket entry to sit and hav refreshments in such beautiful surroundings.

Brockwell Lido

Brockwell Park, Dulwich Road, London SE24 0PA 020 7274 3088

Endearingly known as Brixton's Beach, this historic Lambeth venue has a friendly relaxe atmosphere. It has a 50 meter outdoor pool surrounded by a superb Grade II listed art dec building which houses the gym and studios. Outside is a modern café and changing facilitie with lockers.

Charlton Lido

ornfair Park, Shooters Hill Road, London SE18 4LX 0208 856 7389

he Cafeteria and Sun Terraces are now open along with the 50m outdoor heated pool. A perfect
ace to refuel and relax after your workout or even just to appreciate the views of the park

Hampstead Mixed Pond

he Hampstead Ponds or Highgate Ponds are three large freshwater swimming ponds — two
esignated single sex, and one for mixed bathing — fed by the headwater springs of the River Fleet
- in Hampstead Heath, North London.

his outdoor bathing area is situated at the lower part of Hampstead, below South Park Hill and
ear the bottom of Pryors Field, it is the third of three bathing Ponds in the this area. The Ponds
ite back to the 17th century and were mainly manmade and lined with clay.

Tooting Bec Lido

ooting Bec Road, London SW16 1RU

his wonderful Lido is an open-air fresh water swimming pool in South London. It is the second
rgest swimming pool by surface in the United Kingdom, being 100 yards long and 33 yards wide.
 generally opens the first week in May until the end of September.

Hampton Heated Open Air Pool

igh Street, Hampton, Middlesex TW12 2ST 020 8255 1116

his pool is situated in two acres of woodland next to Royal Bushy Park. The main pool is 36
etres long with a learner pool for children and their parents.

has a colourful History dating back to 1891 with the first proposals for a floating swimming bath
 the river. After many wrangles the pool was eventually opened in 1922.

From 1922 to 1980 the pool was run by various levels of local government as an unheated ope
air pool. In 1981 Richmond Council decided that it was no longer financially viable and it sad
closed. Fortunately for us and which is so often the case, a local community action group w
formed, and in 1984 it was successful in preventing the demolition of the pool. These groups rea
are our nations unsung heroes.

Hillingdon Sports and Leisure Complex
Gatting Way, Uxbridge, Middlesex UB8 1ES 0845 130 73 24

Formerly known as the Uxbridge Lido, this 50m open air swimming pool was reopened in 20
and is spectacular. The outdoor pool has been restored to it's 1930s glory, complete with cascad
(fountains) at both ends of the pool and a new heated shallow splash pool for the children. The
is plenty of space to sunbathe and it has changing rooms and pool side catering.

Park Road Pools and Fitness (Formerly Hornsey Park Road Pools)
Park Road, London N8 8JN 020 8341 3567

After major redevelopment this outside pool is now open. Please check as to days and times as
is limited at the moment in order to gauge demand from local residents, and the public.

London Fields Lido
London Fields West Side, Hackney, London E8 3EU 020 7254 9038

An 18-year campaign by the London Fields User Group saved this 50-metre lido from demolitic
and it reopened in 2006.

ondon Fields Lido is an impressive 50m Olympic size heated outdoor swimming pool open all ear round. The swimming pool has lane swimming available all day. Facilities also include a café as ell as a large sundeck and sunbathing area.

Oasis Swimming Pools

2 Endell Street, London WC2H 9AG

his central London outdoor heated pool is surprisingly situated in an urban area at the junction tween High Holborn and Shaftesbury Avenue. I have included this Lido, as while some other lidos e known for the bold, clean lines of their art deco architecture, the Oasis uses the buildings ound it to no less striking effect. The office blocks towering overhead appear taller than usual to vimmers looking up, and their shining dark glass windows combine with the sweeping curve of e neighbouring block of flats to give the pool a futuristic cutting edge flair.

he rooftop sun terrace and cafe overlooking the pool attract sizeable crowds, during the summer onths and the sunbathing deck area is truly a hidden oasis, a remarkable space in the heart of ondon.

Parliament Hill Lido

uilt in 1938 and refurbished in 2005, the Grade II-listed Parliament Hill Lido measures a generous metres by 28 metres. It has a stainless steel pool liner (the only one in an outdoor pool in the K) which gives the water a metallic shimmer – not that you'll be able to tell when it's packed full people on a sunny day. The lido is unheated, but wetsuits are permitted at the lifeguard's discretion. ere are two sessions a day (7-9am and 10am-6pm) with an additional adults-only evening session Mondays, Thursdays and Fridays. There's a paddling pool for under-fives and a cafe.

Ruislip Lido

Hillingdon (situated between Ruislip Common, Ruislip Woods, and Poors Field)

Ruislip Lido is in fact a reservoir, but this 60-acre water expanse resembles a calm lake. It h artificial sandy beaches and a narrow gauge railway around it. It is all very picturesque and yc could easily be in a sunny cove in Devon instead of the London Borough of Hillingdon. The faciliti include a Woodland Centre, Public toilets (includes disabled facilities and baby changing units.

Play areas with the mini gauge railway and The Waters Edge Pub and Restaurant alongside the ca and restaurant on the beach side are managed by the LBH. All in all on a nice day, decked out your 1920s/30s attire, it is all very civilised. Unfortunately at the moment, bathing and swimmir are not permitted in the lake or water splash areas, due to the water analysis, but hopefully in th future it should be allowed again.

The Serpentine Lido

Hyde Park, London W2 2UH 020 7706 3422

Located in Hyde Park, the Serpentine Lido has had over 100 years entertaining locals and visito alike. You can pull up a deckchair and sunbathe while the children splash gleefully in the backgroun

It consists of a 100 metre stretch of the Serpentine and has changing facilities, sun terrace and ca The accompanying paddling pool is a great asset and the Lido Café Bar with waterside tables is th ideal place to enjoy people-watching with a glass of wine.

The Serpentine swimming club is the oldest swimming club in Britain. They swim every day in the lido area between 6:00 am and 9:30 am and also during the famous race on Christmas day.

The Lido is open from 10 - 6pm every day in June, July and August.

During May it is only open on weekends and Bank Holiday

You can rent sun loungers at a reasonable price for the day, so just pack up your basket of 'goodies'.

Wetsuits are permitted here and the water is tested weekly to ensure quality and safety, which is reassuring if you have younger children in tow.

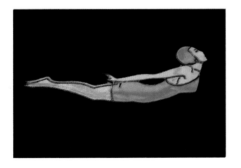

LONDON PLACES OF INTEREST

Out and About in London

When I am in London, I always like to take the pocket A-Z guide, it is so weathered and worn an holds much sentiment with me. I will always be thankful to Phyllis Pearsall who designed this boc during the 1930s.

She was unemployed at the time, and very frustrated trying to find streets for prospectiv employers, using the only available big and bulky maps of the time. What a forward thinking lae

to come up with this ingenious idea.

My daughter prefers to use her A-Z app on her iphon which is just as indispensable to her but just rememb though, it was Ms Pearsall who was the instigator.

It is necessary to know that this is not a totally definitiv guide to every Art Deco building in London and Britai as they are spread far and wide in Greater London an the width and breath of Britain. It is practically impossib to list the entirety as many are private dwellings not ope to the general public. If you do visit some of the privat residential properties, please be mindful and alway respect the owner who may not appreciate someon loitering outside with a camera, so I have mainly on listed those for available for public viewing.

Here, I have condensed in my view the most rewardir and easily accessible sights in London. They are ofte gargantuan in size, but go easily unnoticed by malaise tourists and commuters alike.

Oxo Tower

Bargehouse St, South Bank, London SE1 9PH 020 7803 3888 1928-29 Architect Albert Moore

The famous OXO design windows are a retort from Liebig who wanted to erect illuminate advertising signs but the requests were refused.

Positioned on the South Bank of the River Thames, this iconic building was originally constructe as a power station, until it was acquired in the 1920s by the Liebig Extract Meat Company, th manufacturers of Oxo beef stock cubes. During 1928-29 it was partially rebuilt and redesigned the Art Deco style by the company architect Albert Moore.

The tower was then built with four sets of three vertically aligned windows, which just happene to be in the shapes of a circle, a cross and a circle!

It has an impressive Restaurant on the 8th floor, and a public viewing gallery.

Adelaide House

ing William Street, London EC4 Built 1925 Architects Tate & Partners

This is impressive cube building, which deserves to be admired from the other side of the road t be truly appreciated. It has a warmed stoned exterior with recurring carved stonework, with som Egyptian influences. Adelaide House was groundbreaking at the time as it was the first building i the City to have the steel frame technique that was later mostly employed for skyscrapers aroun the world. It is now the premises of a law company.

Daily Express Newspaper Office

120 Fleet Street, London EC4.   Designed 1932 Architects Ellis and Clark

The gleaming black façade with rounded corners in vitrolite and clear glass, complemented b chromium strips, is cutting edge in design of 'streamline moderne'. The interior is just as impressiv (sadly only accessible to employees and invited guests). The lobby, designed by Robert Atkinso has spectacular silver and gilt decorations, with a dazzling silvered pendant lamp and an ov staircase. Eric Aumonier was responsible for the foyer plaster reliefs. In the past the foyer ha been open to the public on 'London Open House' days, so it is well worth keeping an 'eye out' fc any special open days. The building is now home to Goldman Sachs.

BBC Broadcasting House

Portland Place
London W1
1931-2
Sculptor Eric Gill

When approaching this imposing building, you know that you will be in for a treat. It takes time to really appreciate the size and sculptures above the main entrance: that of Prospero who is being sent out into the foreboding world by his master, Ariel. On the east side of the building are other reliefs and then the huge glass façade of the modern BBC centre, which juxtaposes so well with the 'old and new deco' of the times.

Selfridges Department Store

400 Oxford Street, London W1A 1AB
Architects R.F. Atkinson with D. Burnham supervised by Sir John Burnet.

When you are meandering along Oxford Street be sure to look for the ornamental 11 foot high 'Queen of Time' (c. 1925) which stands above the main entrance. Inside you will also find a brass commemorative floor medallion. Both are by sculptor G W Bayes, RA.

The National Audit Office (previously Imperial Airways)

157-197 Buckingham Palace Road, London SW1 1937-39 Architect Albert Lakeman

This building has an impressive sculpture by E.R. Broadbent of two winged figures wrapping round the world, which is placed above the former terminal entrance. Well worth a visit to see this exquisite art work.

Abbey National Building Society

Abbey House, Baker Street, London W1 Built 1932 Architect J.J. Joass

One not to miss is Abbey House. It has a grand Portland stone block façade with an approximately 30ft high lighthouse which has an intermittently flashing lamp. It also has an impressive clock tower. The fictional detective Sherlock Holmes of 221B Baker Street, created by Sir Arthur Conan Doyle, supposedly lived here.

Shell-Mex Co Building

80 Strand and Victoria Embankment, London WC2 Built 1931 Architect Messrs Joseph.

This gargantuan building ten stories high resembles a giant mantel clock. It is fashioned in Portland stone. It boasts of being London's largest clock and it is wonderful to admire from across the river and close up.

Barkers Department Store

Kensington High Street, London W8 1937-1938

This building has two bronze and glass towers, and a low-relief montage on one of the twin glass towers is futuristic in style. It depicts a V-wing aeroplane with jet engine.

There are also images of an airship, under which an LMS Pacific locomotive heralds forth, with various household goods stacked below.

Bronze spandrels around the building include motifs of cricket pads and stumps, an armchair, a pair of gloves and a selection of ladies shoes.

Battersea Power Station

88 Kirtling Street, London SW8 5BN

Stroll along the embankment and you cannot miss the impressive 113m high building which is decommissioned coal-fired power station located on the south bank of the River Thames.

London Underground Headquarters

55 Broadway, Westminster, London
Built 1929 Architect Charles Holden

Designed by Charles Holden (who designed Southgate tube station), this building was the headquarters of the Underground Electric Railways Company of London. We now know it as the London Underground Headquarters. The building has a clean and simple design, featuring four blocks of offices which radiate from a central tower. In 1929 it won a London Architectural Medal from the Royal Institute of British Architects. It has an array of sculptured commissioned art work, depicting Day & Night, by Jacob Epstein, West Wind by Henry Moore, and various other wind themed deco styled carvings in Portland Stone by renowned artists. The building is now being transformed into luxury apartments.

Hoover Building Perivale

Old Hoover Building, Western Avenue, Greenford, Greater London UB6 8DW
1933 Architects Wallis, Gilbert & Partners

This glorious building started life as a factory for the Hoover Company. It is most impressive in size and structure, with a large tower and two smaller twin towers at the entrance. It has bright orange and green decoration to the towers and a sweeping white façade. Since 1980 when Tesco supermarket took over the rear ground floor, the exterior has remained true to the Art Deco period. During the Second World War it was used to manufacture electrical equipment for tanks and planes.

Sir John Betjeman summed it up by saying it resembles 'a sort of Art Deco Wentworth Woodhouse [large listed country house in Yorkshire] — with whizzing window curves….. derived from Eric Mendelssohn's work in Germany, and splashes of primary colour from the Aztec and Mayan fashion at the 1925 Paris Exhibition'. (English Architecture, Penguin 1974, p.98).

London Zoo

Regent's Park, London NW1 4RY
020 7449 6200 1934 Architects Tecton Designed by Berthold Lubetkin

The Penguin Pool is the place to head for. The Penguins have a famous spiral ramp in a very innovative modernist design which still stands out today. It used reinforced concrete and went 'hand in hand' with the playful, yet elegant nature of the black and white creatures. Agatha Christies Poirot met one of his mysterious clients at this location in 'The Incredible Theft' drama.

Palladium House (formerly known as Ideal House)

Corner of Great Marlborough Street and Argyll Street, London
1928-9 Architects Raymond Hood & Gordon Jeeves

You certainly will not miss the striking black granite with it colourful enamel trimmings as you approach the Ideal House. It was constructed in the late 1920s as the American National Radiator Company's main headquarters. The company had chosen black and gold as the livery colour and decided to incorporate it entirely for the building. You can see the Egyptian influences in the colourful decorated laid champleve (enamel work in which hollows made in a metal surface are filled with coloured enamels) design. It has seven floors and and dominates the surrounding buildings with its beauty.

Carreras Cigarette Factory

Greater London House, 180 Hampstead Road, London NW1 7AW
1928 Architects M.E and O.H. Collins & A.G. Porri

Being designed just four years after the discovery of Tutankhamen's tomb, it is not surprising to see such an astonishingly and highly embellished building. The building which is mainly white has amazing Egyptian style motifs all over. At the time is was very much in 'vogue' among the art deco architects to incorporate the new Egyptian theme, which was reflected in jewellery and fashion. It has two large, very appealing black cats guarding the entrance.

Eltham Palace London

Opened in 1930 Architect Rolf Engstromer

You can immerse yourself in mesmerising style, at this unusual, outstanding Art Deco shrine. It w acquired by the wealthy American couple, Stephen and Virginia Courtauld in 1933. It was origina the childhood home of Henry VIII, and has some of the finest examples of Art Deco architecture England.

The stunning entrance hall, along with the marvellous panelled dining room and luxurious bathroo where Virginia Courtauld has an indulgent gold plated bathroom, live up to the extremes of th decadent era. Two Poirot dramas were partly filmed in the grand entrance hall: that of 'Three A Tradegy' and 'Death on the Nile'.

Florin Court

Charterhouse Square
Clerkenwell
London EC1

This is much better known as Whitehaven Mansions to Agatha Christies fans; being the residence of Hercule Poirot. The impressive privately owned apartments were designed by the architects Guy Morgan in 1936.

It has a beautiful curved façade built using specially made bricks on a wire frame, and a ziggurat roofline. It also has the classic art deco curved base to the steps that lead to the entrance which has iconic cloud ironwork.

Art Deco Underground Stations

The Art Deco Underground Stations are fascinating to see and many will feel very familiar as they are often used for backdrops for period television dramas. You could spend a day or two just visiting these alone. I have chosen the most visually impressive, with striking modernist sharp lines or drum shaped ticket halls. It was Harry Beck who in 1931 designed the new underground iconic map system, with the distinctive circuit board look.

Piccadilly Underground station is in the roundel style. It may look rather tired now, but you can still enjoy the tiled columned features and Art Deco lighting. Others of note are:

Perivale Underground Station
Horsenden Lane Greenford
Middlesex UB6 7NP
1938-47 Architect Brian Lewis

Oakwood Underground Station
Bramley Road
Greater London N14 4UT
Architect Charles Holden

Southgate Underground Station
Station Parade Southgate
Greater London N14 5BH
1932-3 Architect Charles Holden

Cockfosters Station
Cockfosters Road Barnet
Herfordshire EN4 ODZ
1933 Architect Charles Holden

Chiswick Park Station
Bollo Lane
London W4 5NE
1932 Architect Charles Holden

Park Royal Station
Wester Avenue Greater London W5 3EL
1935-6 Architects Herbert Arthur Welch
and Felix Lander

Osterley Station
Great West Road Isleworth
Middlesex TW7 4PU
1934 Architects Charles Holden
and Charles Hutton

Boston Manor Station
Boston Manor Road Brentford
Middlesex TW8 9LQ
1932-34 Architect Charles Holden
and Charles Hutton

Arnos Grove Underground Station
Bowes Road Greater London
N11 1AN
1931-2 Architect Charles Holden

Sudbury Hill Station
Greenford Road Harrow
Middlesex HA1 3RA
1931 Architects Charles Holden
and Stanley Heaps

Sudbury Town Station
Station Approach Wembley
Middlesex HA0 2LA
1931 Architect Charles Holden

Rayners Lane Station
Alexandra Avenue Harrow
Middlesex HA5 5EG
1938 Architects Charles Holden
and Reginald Uren

Eastcote Station
Field End Road Ruislip
Middlesex HA5 1QZ
1939 Architect Charles Holden

Also of interest are Maida Vale Underground Station which was built in 1915 on the Bakerloo Line Edgware, W9, and the precursor to Edward Johnston's iconic underground symbol of 1916-19.

Isokon Building

Lawn Road
Hampstead NW3 2XD
1934 Architect Wells Coats

The Lawn Road flats were astonishing for their time. Not only in the outward architectural style which would have appeared like some science fiction fancy but also in the materials used which was mainly reinforced concrete (the first block of flats built in this way) and the idea of progressive community living for the professional set.

Notable people to have lived in the flats were Walter Gropius and Marcel Bru. Personally, I thin the Isokon's most famous resident was the crime novelist Agatha Christie, who lived there wit her husband Max Mallowan from 1941 to 1948. When Max volunteered for the RAF Directorat in Cairo in 1942, Christie wrote prodigiously to keep her loneliness at bay.

An interesting exhibition area has been created at this Grade I listed property. It tells the story c this pioneering modernist architecture covering everything from the Isokon furniture, the buildir and the previous colourful occupants. It is open from March to October from 11am to 4pm an is free entry.

SOUTH EAST

Accommodation	78
Restaurants, Bars & Cafes	88
Theatres & Cinemas	95
Lidos	101
Places of Interest	105

SOUTH EAST ACCOMMODATION

St Giles House Hotel

41-45 St Giles Street, Norwich, Norfolk NR2 1JR
01603 275180 www.stgileshousehotel.com Architect George Skipper

The beautiful Art Deco style Foyer with wooden curvilinear desk and black and white tiling with columns greets you when entering this elegant hotel with 24 bedrooms and suites. It has a Stylish deco themed bar and restaurant and the 1920s influences merge perfectly with the baroque designed exterior. The architect was also responsible for the Royal Arcade (see section on restaurants & places of interest) and Jarrold's Department store, 1-11 London Street, Norwich, NR2 1JF. The glorious panelled wood walnut suite with domed ceiling and chandelier can be used for functions and is well worth a look around.

Little Stints Holiday Apartment

Old Hunstanton, Norfolk www.ownersdirect.co.uk

Centrally situated in Old Hunstanton, in a quiet secluded location which is nestled away in the art deco styled building of Ashley Gardens you will find Little Stints. All laid out on one level, this well equipped ground floor apartment is double glazed and centrally heated: especially nice for a cozy winter break. It is jolly good for taking your 'faithful friend' with you, as it is pet friendly and the sandy beach on your doorstep is just perfect. It has one bedroom and sleeps 2 to 4 people. The full address is available from the website.

Seaspray House

Sheringham, Norfolk 01263 715779 www.norfolkcottages.co.uk Property Ref: 1450

Seaspray is a lovely large town house which is built in the art deco style, and is set amongst similar properties within a crescent. It has stunning views overlooking the sea, and is within easy reach of lots of quaint shops and restaurants in this unspoilt seaside resort. The accommodation is set over three levels and it sleeps 8 people.

The Aviator Hotel

ywell Aerodrome, Northampton NN6 0BN 01604 642111 www.aviatorhotel.co.uk

his hotel is the full package, as it is an original hotel for the aerodrome. You instantly step back to
he exciting 1930s where the rich and famous would spend a night prior to or arriving back from
olidaying on the continent. The art deco hotel has 50 en-suite rooms of which many have art deco
tyle furnishings and fittings. The restaurant has art deco features and serves a delicious menu.

ou also have the Sywell Aviation Museum based in the lovely art deco surroundings of the
erodrome which charts the history of aviation in Northamptonshire. Spending a weekend or mid
eek break here with all the ambience and facilities really is stepping back in time.

Bethany Art Deco House

altdean Sussex www.crown-gardens.co.uk Architects Connell, Ward & Lucas

his luxurious original art deco detached property which is available for holiday lettings is only
inutes away from Brighton & Hove. It has two bedrooms and two bathrooms and is situated
ery near to the beach.

he interior has a high spec with en-suite wet room, period style bathroom and slipper bath all
rranged on the ground floor level. The open plan living area and kitchen are situated on the upper
rst floor level which is divided by a glass balustrading and steps down to a large spacious lounge
hich is adorned with a glass rectangular dining table. Two French doors open onto the balcony.
urther details and the address are available via Crown Gardens website.

Manor Road Garage
The Pit Stop

ast Preston, Arundel, West Sussex
1282 845052 www.bookcottages.com

his grade II listed petrol station has
ympathetically been converted to a two
edroom art deco apartment which is part
f a complex and is available for hire. It is
rade II listed and up until 1973 was still in

operation. It has plenty of amenities, with a ground floor of living room and dining room/kitchen, with partially open-tread stairs to first floor leading to the bedrooms one double with en-suite and one twin with en-suite.

It is only a 10 minute stroll from the beach and is an ideal location to stay if you are attending Goodwood Revival in September or the Racecourse; come to think of it, any excuse is worth staying at this unique location. (Property ref. 27576).

The Walpole Bay Hotel

Fifth Avenue, Cliftonville, Margate, Kent CT9 2JJ
01843 221 703 Built 1914 extended in 1927

This hotel has been in the Bishop family since 1995. Prior to this Louisa Budge who had it built i 1914 stayed here with her family all her life. The hotel has lovingly been kept in the bygone er and has a unique ambience of past decades. It has spacious lounges, an art deco style verand which is flower decked in the summer months and an atmospheric elegant Edwardian restaurar with resident pianist.

To top this, it even has its original 1920s sprung maple dance floor in the ballroom. The 1927 Ot Trellis gated lift serves all five floors. Described as a living Museum by its owners and packed wit authentic memorabilia this hotel truly is remarkable. It has been used for many filming sets ove the years so you may even find yourself familiar with some of the rooms. Its close proximity t many of Margate's super attractions such as the Shell Grotto and the Dreamland funfair make th an ideal place to stay.

Pink House

Lonsdale Avenue, Margate, Kent CT9 3BY
www.scoot.co.uk Built 1937

The Pink House is a fabulous example of 1930s architecture. It has a lovely large light living/dinir room with three walls of windows including French doors onto the sunny terrace and a jav dropping huge circular window. There is a generous hall with study area, kitchen and downstair cloakroom. Upstairs are three bedrooms and a bathroom and separate loo. The front bedroo has a wall of windows offering sea glimpses and a door to the wrap-around balcony. It has a ver comfortable king-size bed sourced from the Savoy hotel and original built-in wardrobes and bedsid tables.

Priory Bay Hotel

Priory Drive, Seaview, Isle of Wight PO34 5BU 01983 613146

This is a country house hotel which has nuances of art deco in some of the rooms which have wood panelling and furnishings. It has that old world charm and gentleman's club feel with good old fashioned values and excellent service with observant but unobtrusive staff. Being set in 60 acres it really makes you feel as if you are the master of your own country estate in the 1930s. It also has a lovely outside swimming pool.

Control Tower B&B

Bunkers Hill, Egmere, Walsingham
Norfolk NR22 6AZ
01328 821574
www.controltowerstays.com

This original WW2 control tower from 1941 has been lovingly restored and furnished and fitted with an art deco interior.

It has 3 guest rooms, 'The Signal Room' is a large double with an original art deco sumptuous green en suite bathroom and art deco furniture. 'The Boardroom' has an original pink suite with rainfall shower and deco furnishings.

The smaller double is 'The Controllers Rest Room' which also has a rainfall shower.

The delicious and filling vegetarian breakfast is served in the dining room, which is surrounded deco period pieces. I particularly like it that the owner's state that you won't find TVs, trous presses, rashers of bacon and high-tech gizmos. This is my kind of place!

Who'd A Thought It

Headcorn Road, Grafty Green, Nr Lenham, Kent ME17 2AR
01622 858051 www.whodathoughtit.com

This luxurious boutique hotel with restaurant and bar offers opulent rooms. The Roederer Cris Room is extra large and in the Art Deco style, with tiled bathroom and glitzy chandeliers. Clea with a cream white interior and even a circular hot tub on the private patio area. Just perfect f that indulgent deco escape.

Paskins Hotel

3/19 Charlotte Street, Brighton
East Sussex BN2 1AG
01273 601203 www.paskins.co.uk

Paskins Hotel is a wonderful little escape. The interior is decked out in deco style; the dining room has selected furnishings and fittings along with an art nouveau reception area.

Dotted about in the other rooms you will also find influences of the glamorous age. They also have high environmental ethics and top marks for the vegetarian and vegan options on the menu.

Hotel Continental

29 Beach Walk, Whitstable, Kent CT5 2BP 01227 280280 www.hotelcontinental.co.uk

The exterior is in Art Deco style with a white façade with blue detailing. The larger front facing rooms have lovely sea views and are well worth booking. The interior has had a total refit and refurbish in contemporary modern style, The Bistro has a varied French style menu, sourcing local ingredients.

Brooklands Hotel

Brooklands Drive
Weybridge
Surrey KT13 0SL
01932 335700
www.brooklandshotelsurrey.com
Built 2010
Architect Mike Harris

In Art Deco style, especially the foyer, the hotel has modern contemporary style bedrooms. With 120 guest rooms it has been designed around the legacy of the 1930s Brooklands racetrack that surrounds and runs through the building.

It is pretty amazing in design and reflects art deco in style inside and out. It is sleek, luxurious and makes you feel like you are a VIP. All the rooms and suites are superb but I particularly like the panoramic suites with balconies.

Photo by Hufton & Crow © careyjones

Holiday Inn Express

Tothill Street, Minster, Kent CT12 4AU 0871 423 4896 www.hiexramsgate.co.uk

The Holiday Inn Express with 105 rooms is housed in an art deco listed building with leanings to marine architecture (brow of a ship and funnel with arched ceilings). The interior has well chosen modern contemporary furnishings which fit in well with the overall theme of the hotel.

The Whitehouse B&B

02 Minnis Road, Birchington, Kent CT7 9NX
1843 847681 www.minniswhitehousebandb.co.uk

This lovely art deco B&B is a short walk from the gorgeous Minis Bay. It has feature rooms namely 'oirot' a large room with full length patio doors leading to a small balcony facing the front and the 'Hastings' room which has a king size bed and again full length patio doors which lead to a small Alcony facing the back garden.

Springwood Guest House

3 Massetts Road, Horley, Surrey RH6 7DS 01293 775998
www.springwoodgatwick.co.uk

Springwood is an art deco themed bed and breakfast accommodation in the leafy conservation area of Horley and caters for adults nly. Being located only 1.7 miles from Gatwick Airport it is very convenient for a stay and park package. Alternatively it is only half an hour from London and Brighton and is a good base to use if you are thinking of visiting these cities.

The Old Café Holiday Home

Lee-over-Sands
St Osyth
Essex CO16 8EX
01255 820564
www.homeaway.co.uk

This three bed roomed property which can accommodate eight people is set in a rural idyll with spectacular sea views. Art deco inspired it is close to the beach yet in the middle of a large swathe of farmland. It is the perfect place to get away from it all, whilst still being close enough to the local town for social activities.

Ramada Hotel

St Albans Rd West, Hatfield, Hertfordshire AL10 9RH
01707 252400 www.ramada.co.uk Built 1936 Architect E B Musman

Formerly the Comet Hotel this art deco designed building with the Comet Brasserie & Bar ha changed little from when Musman designed it to reflect the iconic de Havilland Comet aeroplan At the time the de Havilland airfield and aircraft factory were located opposite the hotel. Th interior has art deco flourishes but is mainly contemporary modern. The larger executive room are well designed.

viator Hotel

5 Farnborough Road, Farnborough, Hampshire GU14 6EL 01252 555890 www.aviatorbytag.com

his airport designed hotel, created by TAG Group, was opened in 2008 and is a monument to
odern design. It has been designed and created with no expense spared, as the interior with its
·t deco influences of plush leather furnishings, walnut panelling and leather accented furniture
·eates a seductive timeless glamour of aviation. One Eleven is an informal dining room, Brasserie
 for fine dining and the Sky Bar overlooks the TAG owned private airport, as this hotel caters for
lite travellers from London en route overseas. It is a 5 minute walk from the Farnborough Air
ciences Trust Museum and a 9 minute drive to Farnborough Airport.

SOUTH & EAST RESTAURANTS, BARS & CAFES

Café Rouge

29 Hollywell Hill, St Albans,
Hertfordshire AL1 1HD
01727 832777
www.caferouge.com
Built 1931 Architects Percival Blow

This distinctive art deco building which is now home to Café Rouge French Restaurant was once an exhibition hall for Samual Ryder (later to be known for his golfing connections and subsequent Ryder Cup). He originally started business selling seeds in packets and as his business rocketed he needed somewhere for visitors to view the goods, hence he had this building constructed.

It is very aesthetically pleasing with a half cylindrical roof with an excellent ambience for dining.

Ther is now a French restaurant serving a delicious all-day menu of classic French dishes with a contemporary twist.

Metrodeco

38 Upper St James Street, Brighton
Sussex BN2 1JN
01273 677 243
www.metro-deco.com

This lovely tea room has a 1930s feel and glamour. It serves delicious teas or cocktails and is set amongst a room of antiques all of which are for sale. Sheer decadence: you cannot help but be seduced by the sumptuous surroundings and food.

Embankments Bar & Restaurant

River Medway, Mill Street, Rear Archbishops Palace, Maidstone, Kent ME15 6YE
0300 689 7888 www.embankments.moonfruit.com

This floating restaurant which looks like it has just sailed out of the 1930s with wood panelled exterior and round porthole windows is a real treasure. Check out the live music nights, but equally nice is a long lunch on this permanently moored nostalgia trip.

Nags Head Pub

16 Dunmow Road, Bishops Stortford, Hertfordshire CM23 5HP
01279 654553 www.mcmullens.co.uk/nagsheadbishophsstortford Built 1936 Architect E.B. Musman

This delightful art deco pub with dark wood furnishing throughout and modern contemporary interior design is very individual as you don't come across many distinctively art deco pubs in Britain. It is part of the McMullens chain of hostelries.

The Regal Restaurant

38-39 St Andrew's Street, Cambridge CB2 3AR 01223 366459

This purpose built cinema (1937) is now The Regal Restaurant is part of the JD Wetherspoon chai
It fortunately still resembles the cinema inside and out as it has sympathetically been renovate
still retaining some of the original art deco features. The building also houses the Art House Cinem
on the upper floor, accessible via the side entrance doors.

Jamie's Italian

21-24 Royal Arcade, Castle Street, Norwich NR2 1NQ 01603 519967 www.jamieoliver.com

Set in the Art Nouveau Royal Arcade where the cusp of pre deco can be viewed at its best, this
a special setting to enjoy a very good meal.

armalades Café

8-19 The Royal Arcade
City Centre
Norwich NR2 1NQ
1603 767047

This café is very close to Jamie Olivers
alian and likewise is set in the
orious Art Nouveau surroundings
ith leanings towards art deco in the
écor.

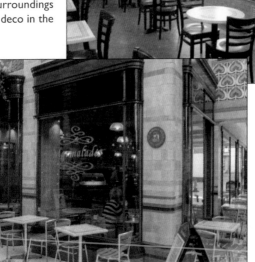

The Peter Cushing Restaurant & Pub

16-18 Oxford Street, Whitstable, Kent CT5
1DD 01227 284100 Rebuilt 1936

Originally built in 1912 as the Oxford Picture
Palace this building was then rebuilt in the art
deco style in 1936 and renamed The Oxford.
It remained as a cinema until 1962 then
functioned as Kings Bingo Hall until 2010.

Fortunately JD Wetherspoon invested a large
amount to sympathetically renovate this
iconic building. It is named after the actor
Peter Cushing as a tribute to him as he
resided in Whitstable.

THE ARLINGTON

Arlington Ballroom

905 Arlington Road, Leigh on Sea
Near Southend, Essex SS9 3LL
Built 1920s
01702 711350
www.arlintontonballroom.co.uk

he building dates back to the roaring 20s 'Art Deco' and 'Jazz' era. It was originally built as a music all, where local residents could dance and listen to live music. Over the years, The Arlington has ad various owners, changing hands many times, yet never quite reaching it's former glory days.)ver time, it had lost its charm and become quite tired, until local businessman and former British European Karate International Champion, William Verner and his wife Susan stumbled across the reary building in late 2012. Due to their family affiliations within the ballroom and latin dancing orld they saw the potential to re-invent the establishment and return it to its former dance hall ory.

hey also made use of their eldest daughter Anna, Art Director for the BBC, helping them to re-esign the space into a truly 'Art Deco' interior. If you look around the local area, you can see eautiful examples of the 1930s streamline architecture in place already, especially buildings such s Argyll House on the seafront. The family have not only brought back to life a piece of local eritage, but also kept the design heritage of the local area too.

'he space also boasts a sweeping staircase up to a mezzanine level, where perhaps a VIP area, jazz uartet or pianist might tickle your fancy. The luxurious bar area and lobby looks out onto the allroom.

he Arlington can also cater for many other events, such as celebrations of any kind, fashion shows nd screenings. The space is there to be enjoyed, and can be considered nothing short of an asset ɔ the local area as not only a stylish piece of heritage architecture and design, but a cultural hotspot ɔo. I have known this building over many decades and it is a joy now to see it fully reinstated.

East Beach Cafe

Littlehampton, West Sussex BN17 5GB
01903 731903 www.eastbeachcafe.co.uk Built 2007 Architect Thomas Heatherwick

Again poetic licence has prevailed and this café just had to be included. 'Once seen never forgotten' comes to mind and it certainly lives up to expectations. The vision is one of waves and shells or even clouds but then that is my art deco mind working as it has been compared to driftwood or sand dunes.

The surprise element, or shock element for some people, can be compared to what people would have experienced back in the deco heyday when the white asymmetrical buildings sprouted. It is composed of 4 separate pieces of mild steel, which has been allowed to rust then coated to protect it from the prevailing sea weather.

SOUTH EAST THEATRES & CINEMAS

Majestic Cinema

Tower Street, King's Lynn,
Norfolk PE30 1EJ
1553 772603
www.majestic-cinema.co.uk
Built 1928 Architects Carnell & White

This is an Art Deco tour de force with its tower clock and fine interior which was purchased from the Empire Theatre Leicester Square London, by one of the Majestic's owners, Mr Adams, in 1928 when the original Empire was being demolished.

Look out for the painted ceilings, mouldings and stained glass windows, which are a marvel. In 2001 a plan was put forward to demolish the cinema and build a multi screen complex in its place. Fortunately this was declined and now the building is Grade II listed.

Hollywood Cinema

Market Place, Fakenham, Norfolk NR21 9BP
1328 856466 www.hollywoodcinemas.net/fakenham Built 1855 converted 1931

The building started life as the Corn Exchange, and then in 1931 it was converted to a 700 seat cinema. This red brick Victorian cinema which exteriorly can easily be taken as an art deco style building operated until 1976 as the Central Cinema. It was then used as a bingo hall until the 1990s. In 2001 Hollywood Cinema once again reinstated it as a cinema and it is well worth a visit.

The De La Warr Pavillion

Marina, Bexhill on Sea, East Sussex TN40 1DP
Box office 01424 229 111 General 01424 229 100 Built 1935

It was the Earl De La Warr who laid the plaque that can still be seen in the floor of the Pavilion foyer. His visions for a modernist building of world renown for the future prosperity and cultur of the town only lasted until the Second World War when it started to decline. Following a lon campaign it has now been fully renovated and restored and opened its doors again in 2006, much acclaim. It is a Grade I listed property on the seafront and is now packed with a fa programme of national and international quality concentrated around and for the contemporar arts, being host to cinema and live theatre. It also has a delightful café where some scenes of Agath Christies 'ABC Murders' featuring Poirot were shot.

The Odyssey Cinema

166 London Road, St Albans, Hertfordshire
AL1 1PG 01727 453088 www.odysseypictures.co.uk Built 1931

This art deco cinema really has used up its 'nine lives'. Fortunately for us, it is now here to stay. The original cinema on the site was destroyed by fire in 1927. Another cinema was rebuilt on the site and opened in 1931 as the Capitol Cinema. It then reigned supreme as a cinema for over 60 years, but like most stars it faded and was under constant threat of demolition when it closed in 1995. Luckily after a long campaign to save this wonderful monument it was reopened in November 2014.

Arts Picture House

8-39 St Andrew's Street, Cambridge CB2 3AR 0871 902 5720 www.picturehouses.com

This independent cinema located above The Regal Restaurant (JD Wetherspoon) has 3 screens and housed in the original art deco cinema building but on the upper floors accessible via the side entrance to the restaurant.

Rex Cinema

Berkhampsted, Hertfordshire HP4 2FG
1442 877759 www.therexberkhampsted.com Built 1936 Architect David Evelyn Nye

The Rex cinema operated for 50 years until its demise in 1988. It then became derelict and it was not until 2004 that the phoenix rose again, as thanks to a local enthusiast and entrepreneur it was fully renovated and restored to its former glory. The whole experience is one of glamour and luxury. The interior and exterior of this art deco building is an extravagant festival of the very best that the period had to offer.

The Regent Centre

High Street, Christchurch, Dorset BH23 1AS
1202 499199 www.regentcentre.co.uk Built 1931

This cinema and theatre has little changed since its opening. It has high ceilings with ornate flourishes and its own café in the foyer which doubles as an art gallery for the local artists. It has varied events throughout the year: mainstream films, plays, dance events and local amateur productions. It is a darling of a venue and like all the independent theatres and cinemas gratefully receives any added support from volunteers wishing to give their precious time or patrons who are able to give extra support with monetary donations, however small that may be.

Assembly Hall

Stoke Abbott Road, Worthing, East Sussex BN11 1HQ
01903 206206 www.worthingtheatres.co.uk Built 1934 Architect C Cowes-Vosey

This building derives its style from the Scandinavian Modernist Movement with Art Deco overtone
It has two stories and constructed in red brick with a pitched roof. The front façade is detaile
with three art deco style stone masks over sea waves above the first floor pivoting casemen
windows. The foyer has art deco fittings also with a pay box. Abundant art deco features ca
further be found in the main hall in the style of a marine theme of sea horses and star lights, wit
streamlined mahogany panelling.

It is also home to the largest Wurlitzer organ in Europe. The venue has a full programme throughou
the year of concerts, theatre and comedy. It can also be hired for dances and banquets.

Broadway Cinema

Eastcheap
Letchworth Garden City
Hertfordshire SG6 3DD
01462 681088
www.broadway-cinema.com

Built 1936 Architect
Bennett & Bidwell

In recent years this cinema
has undergone extensive
refurbishment inside which

has included developing four further screens whilst still keeping the art deco style in the foyer. Th
exterior is very striking as you can see.

egal Moviplex

4 Hans Place, Cromer, Norfolk NR27 9EQ 01263 510151 www.merlincinemas.co.uk

or nearly 100 years films have been shown on this site. The Cromer Theatre of Varieties, built in 914, was known for showing short silent films between variety acts. Then in 1936 the theatre as modernised, refurbished and enlarged. It has four screens and is the oldest operating cinema Norfolk. It is part of the Merlin chain of cinemas and theatres which are mostly housed in otable buildings. This delightful venue still has the original neon lighting strip outside.

mpire Cinema

elft Street, Sandwich, Kent CT13 9HD 01304 620480 www.empiresandwich.co.uk Built 1937

his cinema still has the original neon lighting and art deco architecture that accommodates 130 eople for mainstream movies and monthly classics. In 1993 it opened its doors to a renovated nd modernised cinema, fortunately retaining its heritage. The Lounge section is situated in the riginal stalls area and has been refurbished with comfortable chairs and tables and a maple dance oor installed in front of the cinema. It has a fully licensed bar.

Theatre Royal

ddington Street, Margate, Kent
T9 1PW
1843 292795
ww.theatreroyalmargate.com

his Georgian theatre is just so dorable, though it lacks the art eco style, that it had to be cluded. The exterior and interior re phenomenal, and it is the erfect ending to a vacation in art eco Margate.

Watford Colosseum

Rickmansworth Road, Watford WD17 3JN

01923 571 102 www.watfordcolosseum.co.uk Built 1938 Architect Charles Coles-Voysey

This building started life as the Watford Town Hall Assembly Room and is a flat roofed box shap
brick and glass building. It can seat 1309 guests and has regular live music and entertainmen
throughout the year. It's also home to a famous Compton organ which has been fully refurbishe
by Watford Borough Council.

Princes Theatre

Station Road, Clacton-on-Sea, Essex CO15 1SE

www.tendringdc.gov.uk/leisure/princes-theatre Built 1926 Architect Sir A Brumwell Thomas

This theatre, which also served as the town hall, is grade II listed. It has a classical brick exterio
and a segmented vaulted ceiling with plaster panelled side walls and decorative tongue flute
balcony facades. The Proscenium has a broad moulded fram and segmental arch. All in all th
theatre is a lovely monument to 20th century architecture.

Century Cinema

129 Pier Avenue, Clacton on Sea, Essex CO15 1NJ

01255 429850 Built 1936 Architect G H B Gould

Over the past few years this cinema has been renovated and refurbished whilst still retaining som
of its original art deco glamour. It has also reverted back to its original name as over the years
has been used for a bingo hall and had many different cinema owners. It has a varied mix of liv
screenings and up to date modern releases.

SOUTH EAST LIDOS

altdean Lido

ltdean Park Road, Brighton, East Sussex BN2 8SP 01273 390116 Architect R W H Jones

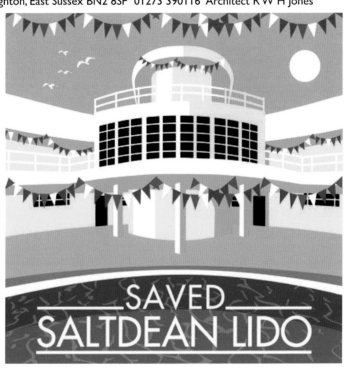

SAVED SALTDEAN LIDO

he marvellous and xciting news is that e shall once again be le to experience is truly remarkable do as funding has en secured to re en this grade II ted swimming pool ith the pool planned open In June 2016. he Community terest Company tends to run the lo site and its cilities on behalf of e community, investing profits ck into this asset for ng term future nerations. Keep up--date with the ogress via their cebook page.

Voodup Outdoor Amenity Pool

llesbury, Essex 01621 869039 tollesburypc@btinternet.com

oodup Pool is a salt water bathing pool with an area of sand at one end. There is also a grassed ea with picnic tables. During the summer months toilet facilities are provided. No lifeguards are attendance, so be extra careful if you are not a strong swimmer or if you are supervising children. ontact information is via Tollesbury Parish Council.

Voburn Open Air Swimming Pool

awley Road, Woburn, Bedfordshire
525 290168 www.prstubbs.btinternet.co.uk/woburn.htm Built 1911

he 11th Duke of Bedford had this lido built for the benefit of his workers which was very much preciated at the time. It is approximately 46 x 23 metres and is generally open daily from late ay to September.

Priory Lido

Priory Street, Ware, Hertfordshire SG12 9AL 01920 460703
www.wareonline.co.uk www.waretowncouncil.gov.uk
Built 1934 Architect R.W. Grantham

This lido is situated in the grounds of Ware Priory on the old orchard area. It was built following a local meeting of the townspeople who agreed to this lovely open air public bathing pool. It is 30 m by 9 m and the changing rooms and showers were added in the 1970s. It is heated and does have qualified lifeguards. As it is situated in the Park area refreshments are available from a nearby kiosk.   The pool is funded through Ware Council and the volunteers Friends of Ware  Lido. Again I doff my hat to all dedicated campaigners who raise funds to keep our heritage alive. This is a beautiful pool in a wonderful setting.

Pells Pool

Swimming Pool, Brook Street, Lewes, East Sussex BN7 2PW 01273 472334 www.pellspool.org.

This outdoor grade II listed 46m pool (built 1860) is fed by a natural spring and is the oldest freshwater open air pool in the country. The present pool tank 46 x 23 metres lies within two previous shells, the oldest being the original. There is a toddlers pool and play area also. The pool is set in a nature reserve by the river and the site is held in trust on behalf of the people of Lewes on land which was bequeathed in 1602.

Letchworth Open Air Pool

Norton Common, Icknield Way, Letchworth,
Hertfordshire SG6 4UF
01462 684673
Built 1935

This heated 50 metre pool also has a paddling pool with a sun bathing area. It is now administered by Hitchin Swimming Centre.

Hitchin Swimming Centre

Fishponds Road, Hitchin, Hertfordshire SG5 1HA 01462 441646 Built 1938

Situated in a park setting this 50 metre outdoor heated pool with sunbathing terrace as well as a 25 metre indoor pool. It is brick built with green glazed roof tiles, fine fountain and a rose pergola. See, www.sll.co.uk for this and other pools.

Wycombe Rye Lido

The Rye, Off Bassetsbury Lane, High Wycombe
Buckinghamshire HP11 1QX 01494 769472

This was formerly the Holywell Mead Outdoor Swimming Pool. It reopened in 2011 following a successful campaign. The pool was built in 1957 but based on a 1930s design. It has a 30 metre outdoor pool with a 20m teaching pool, grass area and patio with sun lounging facilities and a café. It is run by Fusion, who have an investment program for the future.

The Lido is surrounded by The Rye which is High Wycombe's own centre park with an original layout conceived by Lancelot "Capability" Brown with later improvements by Humphrey Repton. It covers an area of more than 22 hectares (53 acres). There was once a Roman villa on The Rye and decorative panels either side of the pool entrance are original Roman walling recovered from the site.

DON'T YOU WISH YOU WERE HERE.

Strand Leisure Park

Pier Road, Gillingham, Kent 01634 573176

Known as The Strand Baths on the river Medway they were built in 1894 by Mr Cucknow A Baker. The pool is 28m long and 14m wide. Recently it has been refurbished, providing lanes, fountains, slides and river ride.

Guildford Lido

Stoke Park
Guildford
Surry GU1 1HB
01483 449108

This 50 metre pool (built 1933) with love
landscaped gardens retains much of its 1930
charm.
It is heated to 23°C, has paddling pools an
water slides and it is situated in Stoke Par
next to Guildford college.

Jesus Green Lido

Chesterton Road, Cambridge CB4 3AX 01223 302579 www.jesusgreenpool.org

This lido (built 1923) is in a marvellous position by the River Cam on the south side. It rank
amongst one of the longest outdoor pools in Europe with a staggering 91 metres in length an
approximately 14 metres wide. It has timber built changing facilities which were constructed in th
1960s. It is well planned as at one end of the pool there is a sloping paved area, ideal for sunbathir
and the other end is a shady bank where you can sit and relax whilst enjoying the beautiful settin
In 2015 a wooden sauna hut was installed for the chilly days. Just outside the pool further facilitie
include a tennis court and children's play area.

SOUTH EAST
PLACES OF INTEREST

City Hall

St Peters Street, Norwich, Norfolk NR2 1NH
Built 1938
Architects Charles H James &
Stephen Rowland Pierce

Norwich is a fine city with its commanding art deco city hall and tall clock tower that has the largest clock bell in the UK. The building also has the longest balcony in England being 112m long. The huge heraldic lions outside the main entrance stand guard over the art deco interior which has original light fittings and a marble floor and columns.

Royal Arcade

City Centre
Norwich
Norfolk
Built 1899
Architect
George Skipper

The impressive 75m covered Royal Arcade near the market place is a sight not to be missed. The wrought iron Art Nouveau canopy and tiled mosaic floor is craftsmanship at

its best. The shops inside the arcade have decorative facades. Cafes and restaurants located within the arcade are also in the art deco style.

Bridewell Museum

Bridewell Alley, Norwich, Norfolk NR2 1AQ
01603 629127
www.museumsnorfolk.org

This fine museum is home to a large collection of old shoes, all manufactured in Norwich. There is also a recreation of a 1930s pharmacy, one of the most complete examples in the country. A delightful time can be whittled away in this old part of the City.

Deco Days

37 St Giles Street, Norwich, Norfolk NR2 1JN 01603 633364

This delightful shop is dedicated to selling original high quality Art Deco items which inclue furniture, lighting, glassware, ornaments and many more objets d'art. It really is a hidden gem Norwich and only a few doors down from St Giles Hotel. The friendly knowledgeable shop own is only too willing to guide you through the individual pieces.

Baron Art

17 Chapel Yard, Holt, Norfolk NR25 6HG 01263 713430

This colourful Art Deco shop specialises in original high quality ceramics, figurines and paintings. It not to be missed when visiting this upmarket fashionable town, packed with antique and vinta; shops.

Deco Debenham

2 High Street, Debenham, Suffolk IP14 6QW 01728 860477 www.decodebenham.com

Housed in an ancient Foresters Hall of 1905 you will find this a beautiful haven of original Art Deco furniture and fitting accessories. It is like walking around a 1930s film set - absolutely captivating.

Hunstanton

North Norfolk

Hunstanton has a conservation area which has been extended on the west side of the main road to include the pleasant 'Art-Deco' style shops (Nos 1 to 5) and the 'Coal Shed' gallery behind. This little building is a survivor of the railway complex – a coal depot office which stood in the station yard.

Empire Theatre

Blackfriars Road, Wisbech, Cambridgeshire PE13 1AT Built 1932 Architect Ward & Woolnough

The Empire Theatre is a grade II listed building and is a fine example of Art Deco architecture. The artificial stone Deco exterior has geometrical glazing bars to the windows which rise up to the shaped pinnacle at the centre. The foyers and auditorium are remarkably complete with impressive plaster decoration and beautifully inlaid doors. The proscenium arch is angular with adornments which are flanked by clustered organ pipes and recessed boxes. Stylised Aztec plaques adorn the balconies, along with the tall canted bay window and Art Deco pinnacle. It is now a bingo hall.

The Spirella Building

Bridge Road, Letchworth Garden City, Hertfordshire SG6 4ET 01462 476694

This former corset factory was totally renovated and tastefully restored in 1996. It now houses over 20 different enterprises and businesses and houses the spectacular Spirella Ballroom. Throughout the year the ballroom with its curved ceiling and art deco features including large porthole windows, hosts different entertainment programmes, including dance classes.

Dreamland Amusement Park

Marine Terrace, Margate, Kent CT9 1XJ
www.dreamland.co.uk
Architects Julian Leathart & WF Granger for
John Henry Iles, Dreamland Entertainment

Dreamland amusement park was first used for amusement rides in 1880, although the Dreamland name was not used until the 1920s.

Fortunately for us following much uncertainty over the years it reopened in June 2015 following a 12 year campaign to save the attraction, which is the oldest surviving amusement park in the UK. The Dreamland Trust is the organisation that originated the project, secured funding from organisation including Save Dreamland Campaign, Heritage Lottery Fund, Thanet District Council and Sand Heritage Ltd. Every attraction is here to transport you back to traditional seaside entertainment which includes the gallopers, dodgems and teacup rides. There is a bandstand and a beautiful an sympathetically restored 1933 ballroom. The grade II listed ballroom called 'Hall By The Sea' is availabl to hire and is multi functional as the stage is adaptable. It hosts shows, concerts and parties bot private and corporate throughout the year. Look out for dances and cabarets as this marvellous spac comes alive when the music starts. The entrance to the ballroom is located to the right of the ma amusement building with separate entry points allowing its use independently or as a whole.

Dreamland Cinema

Marine Terrace, Margate, Kent Built 1934 Architects Julian Leathart & WF Granger

It was reassuring news that in August 2015, Thanet Borough Council announced that Dreamlan cinema had been secured with a government grant of £1.8 million for restoration which include work on the metal lettering, new neon lighting, windows shop front and restoration to the fasci The Sunshine Café will also be restored with a new roof and fascia. Thankfully this is a succes story so we can all enjoy this iconic art deco cinema in the future.

Palm Bay Avenue
Cliftonville, Margate

Here you will find fine examples of art deco houses and apartments dotted around this area. The Palm Bay estate is a 1930s architect-designed estate with strict planning rules to ensure the highest quality build. It is a genteel residential area which has a nice old fashioned parade of shops and the beach has a permanent seawater swimming pool.

Margate Museum
Market Place, Margate, Kent CT9 1ER 01843 231213

You will find that the museum has archive facilities which will allow you to explore Margate's former art deco cinemas, amongst other material relating to Dreamland Amusement Park.

Shoreham Airport
Cecil Pashley Way, Shoreham-by-Sea, West Sussex BN43 5FF 01273 467373

This airport saw its first flight in 1910 by Harold Plume Piffard, who famously completed a mid air turn. It was not until circa 1935 that the iconic Art Deco terminal building was designed by Stavers Hessell Tiltman. Pleasure flights are available to suit all budgets, and the whole experience of this living art deco airport is a pleasure beyond words.

Princes Canning Factory
85-87 Lynn Road, Wisbech, Norfolk Built 1923

This Art Deco Building built by the Smedley family is Grade II listed. It consists of an adjoining pair of town houses and is the office block and frontage to the 17 acre site of one of the largest canning factories in the UK. Over the years, it has belonged to many different food processors and fortunately the original Art Deco front has been kept and is vibrantly coloured in white with red detail.

Worthing Pier
Marine Parade, Worthing, West Sussex BN11 3PX 01903 221067 www.visitworthing.co.uk

The original Worthing Pier was destroyed by fire in 1933 and a new pier was built (1935) in the Streamline Modern design with its beautiful contours and curves.

In 1940 the pier was sectioned and a large hole was blown in the pier, to prevent it being used as a landing platform for enemy invasions.

The Pavilion Theatre and Denton Cafe is situated at the northern, land end of the pier; at the middle is the 1935 amusement arcade, whilst the Southern Pavilion at the sea end houses a tearoom and function area. It successfully underwent extensive restoration during 2013/14 and is now a delightful venue for the whole community and visitors to enjoy. The pier is owned by Worthing Borough Council.

Stoke Abbott Court

2 Stoke Abbott Road, Worthing,
West Sussex BN11 1HF

The classic Art Deco façade of these privately owned residential flats is fresh and clean with newly restored paintwork and sympathetic restoration. It now looks fresh as a daisy and well worth a stroll past when visiting Worthing as it is only a short distance from the town centre.

Onslow Court Apartments

Brighton Road, Worthing, West Sussex BN11 2PL Built 1933 Architect A.T.W. Goldsmith

This spectacular Art Deco architecture was originally built as a block of private flats and still remain that to this day. It is in a stunning position offering unrestricted sea views from the sea fro location.

In 1934 it boasted of having centrally heated rooms with constant hot water and fully fitted electr kitchens, fridges, luxurious bathrooms and sun balconies.

Embassy Court

King's Road, Brighton
East Sussex BN1 2PX
Built 1934-36 Architect Wells Coates

This modernist building is an 11 story block of 72 privately owned apartments. It is beautifully proportioned and is situated on the seafront sandwiched between Victorian and regency designed buildings.

Marine Court

Marina, St Leonards-on-Sea
East Sussex TN38 0DZ
Built 1936-38
Architects Kenneth Dalgleish
Roger K Pullen

This gargantuan building which resembles an ocean liner is fourteen storeys high and from basement to roof measures 49 metres in height and 127 metres in length. It has two very different perspectives. When viewed from the Marine Court it appears slim and tall, whereas from the beach the full scale of the building appears to engulf all those on the seafront. The materials used for construction were the pioneering steel frame which was also used at the De La Warr Pavilion at Bexhill-on-Sea. This grade II listed building is now privately owned apartments.

The Homewood

Portsmouth Road, Esher, Surrey KT10 9JL
01372 476424 Designed 1937
Architect Patrick Gwynne

This National Trust property is a spectacular showcase of futuristic Modernist design. The influence of continental avant garde can clearly be seen all around. It has a wonderful spiral staircase, and built-in furniture which conceals a drinks cabinet and gramophone. The gleaming marble and tiny wall tiles made of glass are stunning. All this is situated amidst a glorious woodland garden. The architect designed it for his parents, sister and himself to live in, which they did until his death in 2003. It can be visited on select days between April to October via a guided tour as it is administered by a tenant.

To arrange a
visit contact:
01372 476424

JC Decaux

Head Office, 991 Great West Road, Brentford, Middlesex TW8 9DN
020 8326 7777 Built 1936 Architect F E Simpkins

This former Curry's Ltd Warehouse is an amazing testament to industrial architecture during the art deco period. It is made of reinforced concrete with some steel framing which was needed at the rear. The long office block at the front of the building has a flat roof and to the rear you can see the irregular industrial profile. The rising central storeys have an impressive staircase tower as its centrepiece. It is now home to the French Company JC Decaux one of the largest multinational advertising companies in the World.

Leeds Castle

Maidstone, Kent ME17 1PL 01622 765400

Leeds castle has 900 years of history to share, but if you are an art deco fanatic or just lover of the 1930s, the interior design of the rooms is from that era. The main attraction here for any art deco affionado is that of Lady Baillie's room, with its beautiful original art deco marble bathroom. She was the last private owner of this spectacular castle and was renowned for her lavish house parties and her love of flowers. Her French interior designer Stephane Boudin played a large part in decorating the rooms. The Castle has many themed events throughout the year and offers 'dine and sleep' packages in state bedrooms, battlement bedrooms and stable court yard bedrooms.

SOUTH WEST

Accommodation   114

Restaurants, Bars & Cafes   128

Theatres & Cinemas   132

Lidos   140

Places of Interest   145

SOUTH WEST ACCOMMODATION

Burgh Island Hotel

Bigbury-on-Sea, South Devon TQ7 4BG
01548 810514 www.burghisland.com Built 1929 Architect Matthew Dawson

The history of this art deco grade II listed shrine dates back to when Archibald Nettlefold (of Nettleforld Studios and heir to a substantial engineering firm) bought the Island in 1927. He had the Hotel built on the site of a smaller hotel and had further additions added in the 1930s including a room created from the captain's cabin of the 1821 warship HMS Ganges. It became famous for the celebrity guests who patronised the premises: Noel Coward, Edward and Mrs Simpson, Agatha Christie and the hoi polloi of the day.

The Hotel, is reached at high tide by a distinctive 'sea tractor' as the causeway is tidal, and this all adds to the excitement of your arrival and departure, although when the tide is out it only takes 5 minutes to walk across the causeway.

our difficulty starts when you try to decide which art deco room to stay in! That I cannot answer they are all thrilling in their unique way.

ne furnishings and fittings throughout the whole hotel are all art deco. There are just too many ems to list as it is like being in a sweet shop and wanting to savour every flavour. The exterior of e hotel has a sun terrace which leads down to the Mermaid bathing pool, which is a permanent it tidal naturally protected pool with a jetty to swim out to. This is where you must embrace our vintage swimming attire including bathing cap and take a twice daily dip (not compulsory but ghly recommended).

he hotel was chosen as the setting for Agatha Christie's Evil Under the Sun. She also wrote 'And hen There Were None' whilst staying at the hotel and the moment you step onto the island you ave the 21st century behind and step back to the Jazz Age. This hotel is every deco afionados ream, a true capsule of nostalgia.

Marine Villa

33 Littlestairs Road, Shanklin, Isle of Wight PO37 6HS
07877 036687 www.artdecohouseuk.com   Built 1929 Architect E L Smith

This grand detached house has decadently proportioned rooms with huge stained glass window that bring out the oak-panelled hallway and magnificent staircase and galleried landing. The a

deco furnished rooms are exceptional, with large bedrooms and stunning view overlooking Sandown Bay, it is luxuriou glamour of a bygone age, at its best. Th property sleeps up to 16 adults with the 2 seater dining table ideal for a large fami gathering.

Most of the fixtures and fittings have bee lovingly resurrected from the 1930s, from th beautiful walnut cocktail cabinet in the loung to the stunning wardrobe and dressing tab suite set in bedroom 4.

ere are wonderful cliff top walks around the ouse and a gentle slope takes you down to the each below. The owners who are a jolly decent endly couple are as passionate about art deco as yone can possibly be and nothing is too much ouble for them, when you are staying in their operty which is a stupendous homage to art deco side and out.

urritella

est Wittering, West Sussex. 01243 672217 www.baileys.uk.com

This classic art deco house is situated directly on the beach. It has been fully renovated and lovingly remodelled. It has a roof garden with spectacular views across to the Isle of Wight and along The Solent to Portsmouth. Turritella has a large open plan reception room which includes the kitchen, living and dining area with a spiral stair case leading to a first floor sun room and the first bedroom. It can accommodate 8 people and has 4 bedrooms.

ortland House

) Redcliff View, Weymouth Dorset DT4 8RZ
344 335 1287 Built 1935 Architect Lord G Wellesley & T Wills

is National Trust property has hitewashed rendered walls and a Roman e hipped roof with deep eaves along with o rendered lateral chimneys with pered stacks. It is furnished in Art Deco yle and contains some beautiful original atures and period furniture. It is sitioned on a natural south-facing slope th scenic views. It consists of spacious rraces, one above the other, and most of e sunny rooms with French windows

en directly onto them. The arcaded loggias which are around each corner of the building are rfect for shade in the summer months. This property is available for most of the year and it is solutely wonderful for a large family or friend gathering any season of the year. This National ust Holiday villa has 7 bedrooms and sleeps up to 12 people. Property Ref: 003042.

St Moritz Hotel

Trebetherick, Wadebridge, Cornwall PL27 6SD   01208 862242   www.stmoritzhotel.co.uk

This modern interpretation art deco hotel and apartment complex with 48 rooms can be used a
either a self catering holiday or as a hotel package, it is very flexible. This relatively new building
in the style and design of an art deco property and despite its age still has an authentic feel an
ambience of 1930s, with all the modern luxuries one would expect. The rooms have a spectacul.

utlook over the sea and the Camel Estuary. The front of the building has terraces and balconies nd each lounge in the apartments leads straight out onto this. It is a very relaxing place to stay hilst also having many activities close by. The apartments have two, three or four bedrooms. acilities also include a swimming pool, sauna and steam room, along with restaurants and bar. It eally is a versatile venue in wonderful surroundings.

aunton-Sands Hotel & Restaurant

lorth Devon, Saunton Rd, Braunton, Devon EX33 ILQ 01271 890212 Built 1936

his 92 bedroomed hotel was originally built by Sir John Christie, the founder of the Glynebourne pera, and is an art deco haven as very little has structurally changed since it was built.
 has three restaurants and the main one has the original deco chandeliers and panoramic views ross Saunton Sands. It is a very flexible establishment and guests can either self cater in the partments or reside in the hotel rooms. The facilities with indoor and outdoor pools and umerous sporting activities are superb.

Mullion Cove Hotel

Mullion Cove, Lizard Peninsula, Cornwall TR12 7EP 01326 240328 www.mullion-cove.co.uk

This magnificent hotel was built on the cusp of the 20th Century and is set on a cliff-top on th
Lizard Peninsula overlooking Mullion harbour and fishing cove.

The 30 rooms and suites range in style from traditional to elegant, and the suites have 2 bedroom
and lounge areas. They are all impeccably furnished and particularly special are the Premier room
with sea views and some furnishings in the art deco style. With the sophisticated formal Atlant
View Restaurant and the opulent art deco inspired Glenbervie Bar with bistro style menu plus
guest lounges with sea views this is a very special escape. A heated outdoor pool further enhanc
this turn of the century Palace. It is surrounded by National Trust land and is positioned on th
Cornish coastal path.

Photograph © and courtesy of the Mullion Cove Hot

Riviera Hotel

Bowleaze Cove, Weymouth, Dorset DT3 6PR 01305 836600 Built 1937 Architect L Stewart Smit

You are immediately struck by this striking grade II listed hotel which has iconic art deco arch
and are a local landmark.

It has 98 chalet-style rooms in 1930s art deco style, and a restaurant and outdoor pool and saun
overlooking stunning Dorset scenery. Over 4 million pounds has been invested into the hotel b
the current owners who took over in 2009, completely refurbishing and renovating the propert
making major improvements to its function rooms, bars and leisure facilities. Back in 1937 th
property was reinforced using concrete in the mouchel/hennebique system. This was undertake
by Tuscon Ltd with rendered asphaltic flat roofs. It is now a symmetrical building with a slend
square tower that has a recessed panel to each face with a 'keystone' above with 'Riviera' inscribe
vertically on the panel. In the late 1950s it was owned by Pontins Holiday camp and since then
has continued to operate as a hotel until the current owners have lovingly and thoughtfully breathe
new life into it. It has the Bowleaze Restaurant which offers fine dining in a stunning environmer

Photographs © Riviera Hotel

Cumberland Hotel

7 E Overcliff Drive, Bournemouth, Dorset BH1 3AF
1202 298 350 www.cumberlandbournemouth.co.uk Built 1937

After the war this hotel soon became Europe's largest Jewish Hotel complete with synagogue and remained so for many years. However it did get very tired and needed a complete overhaul. After a large investment, it has been tastefully returned back to its heyday using original materials and patterns looks of the time. It has Italian marble fireplaces and floors with original 1930s patterns used for the carpets.

The floors and ceilings were restored along with the wall panelling, it is sheer heaven. The designers responsible for this marvellous transformation are Micro & Micro of Bournemouth. It has two restaurants, the Ventana Grand Café which combines art deco luxury and contemporary style and the Mirabelle Restaurant, an elegant venue which can seat up to 250 guests.

The hotel can boast of a Miami style outside swimming pool with sun loungers which have direct access to the Ventana Café whereby you can sip your cocktails whilst reading your reading your favourite 1930s Jeeves & Wooster caper!

Ventana Grand café at the Cumberland Hotel

Mercure Bowden Hall

Bondend Road, Upton St. Leonards, Gloucester GL4 8ED
0844 815 9077 www.mercuregloucester.co.uk

You could be fooled when you first see this gleaming white hotel that it is of the art deco period when in fact it is a grade II listed Georgian hall. It is set in 12 acres of beautiful park and woodland and the rooms on the front have views over the lake. It is well worth upgrading to the privilege rooms for the view alone.

The interior is designed and furnished in traditional and contemporary style. It has a Brasserie Restaurant which serves a fine selection of foods. The 'cherry on the top' is the heated indoor pool which has attractive columned gallery area.

Premier Inn

Westover Road
Bournemouth
Dorset
BH1 2BZ

0371 527 8124

Built 1936

Architects
J Seal & Partners

This Premier Inn is situated in a gargantuan Art Deco building which was formerly the Palace Court Hotel which features stylish interiors and a modern restaurant, all with little Deco touches. It has 120 rooms, and the elegant Thyme restaurant, which serves an international menu.

Seaspray House

St Ives, Cornwall 01736 630015 www.carbisbayholidays.co.uk

This luxury single storey art deco style house is positioned on the beach with direct access onto the golden sands of Carbis Bay. It has a decked terrace to admire the panoramic sea views and eat al fresco. It has 2 bedrooms which includes the sumptuously fitted master bedroom. This really is a place to escape the modern day pressures of 21st century living. Further details regarding the address details are available through the letting agents Carbis Bay Holidays.

Tower Hall B & B

Flexford Lane, Sway, Lymington
Hampshire SO41 6DN

07836239733 info@towerhall.co.uk

Described as 'Hampshire's finest folly' this concrete tower was conceived by barrister Andrew Thomas Turton Peterson in 1879 and completed in 1886. He was fascinated by construction and had the idea to build this 218ft high concrete construction to showcase the material alongside a mansion. It cost £30,000 at the time and stands magnificently today as testament to this man's dreams.

There are three delightful rooms with luxury interiors, which are in the main mansion and overlook

the Tower. The dramatic Tower room has a sumptuous en-suite bathroom which has been recreated in an opulent Art Deco style of block glass with a translucent wall and black and white marble mosaic tiled flooring. The bedroom is elegantly decorated and furnished in country house style with a French belle époque influence.

Kaywana Hall B&B

Higher Contour Road, Kingswear, Dartmouth, Devon TQ6 0AY
01803 752200 www.kaywanahall.co.uk Architect Stan Bolt

The owners of this high end bed and breakfast knew they had found something very special when they bought it in the late 1990s. It needed extensive remodelling and now it is cutting edge design. It amalgamates 1960s design along with modern contemporary and art deco influences which join together with the original butterfly architectural design (one of only 4 houses built in Devon with its distinctive butterfly wing shaped roof). It has three beautiful rooms; Beech,

hich overlooks the swimming pool (for summer months) and Oak and Ash which sit at the back
the house with the woodland views. The rooms all have the same facilities, with separate
itrances, decks and mini fridges. All bathrooms have separate showers and baths. It may not be
t deco but with it distinctive use of sharp lines and curves along with the opulence and glamour
at it exudes make it a happy contender to sit comfortably in the deco heyday of architectural
esign.

he Beach House B&B

Boscawen Road, Falmouth, Cornwall TR11 4EL 01326 210407 www.beachhousefalmouth.co.uk

pposite Falmouth's main sandy beach you will find this lovely art deco property. Most of the
ooms have magnificent sea or garden views. The en-suite rooms are all furnished with a crisp and
esh coastal theme.

The Ferryman B&B

16 Victoria Road South, Southsea, Hampshire PO5 2BZ 023 92875824 www.ferryman-hotel.co.u

This bed & breakfast is a little gem and offers such good value. It is in a distinctive 1930 buildi⋮ and the interior has original deco furniture in most of the bedrooms. It is located near to ma⋮ attractions and offers double, twin or family rooms with en suites or bathrooms.

The Yacht Inn

Green Street, Penzance, Cornwall TR18 4AU www.yatchtinn.co.uk 01736 362787

Located on the Penzance seafront this beautiful Art Deco building has 7 rooms, all decorated in contemporary modern style. Most have stunning sea views over Mount's Bay and there is a separa⋮ restaurant which has a delicious menu of locally sourced foods.

Queens Quay

Torwood Street, Harbourside
Torquay, Devon

holidaylettings.co.uk

Queens Quay has eight waterfront apartments with balconies which overlook the harbour side. It was formerly a hotel but now has been sympathetically renovated and has not lost its origin⋮ art deco charm and sophistication. The rooms are light and airy and the balconies are a delight t sit out on and watch the world go by.

The Corbyn Appartments

Torbay Road, Torquay
Devon TQ2 6RH

01803 215595

www.thecorbyn.co.uk

This modern purpose built complex offers one and two bedroomed apartments with spectacular views over Torquay. It is particularly nice in it has an air of art deco scattered throughout with furnishings and décor. Particularly nice is the swimming pool with its trompe l'loeil deco image. It also offers long term lets should you wish to winter over on the English Riviera.

Mercure Brigstow Hotel

Welsh Back 5-7, Bristol BS1 4SP 0117 9292030 www.mercure.com

This 4 star hotel is located in the city centre. I particularly like the modern day take on Art Deco style. The impressive public areas and bedrooms are all curvilinear or asymmetrical and the contemporary furnishings in the 116 guest rooms complement the overall design. The Ellipse restaurant has elegant cuisine and the bar serves delicious cocktails.

SOUTH WEST RESTAURANTS, BARS & CAFES

Glenbevrie Bar

Mullion Cove Hotel, Mullion, Helston , Cornwall TR12 7ER
01326 240328

A perfect spot to enjoy an expertly prepared cocktail, or a long, chilled glass served by th
knowledgeable bar staff. The bar also offers a superb yet less formal dining venue, where classic
such as moules frites or the Mullion Cove Hotel signature Seafood Platter are served. The men
as you would expect, is prepared with produce sourced from the chef's favourite farmers, fisherme
and growers from around Cornwall.

Hyde & Co Bar

2 The Basement
Upper Byron Place
Bristol BS8 1JY

0117 9297007

www.hydeandcobristol.net

This speakeasy style bar has a low lit gentleman's club feel. The décor is an eclectic mix of vintag
and new and a piano sits in one corner. The varieties of classic cocktails, mainly taken from th
prohibition era, are delicious.

Bea's Vintage Tea Room

6-8 Saville Row, Bath BA1 2QP 01225 464552 www.beasvintagetearooms.com

Step back in time when you enter Bea's charming Vintage Tea Rooms next to the Assembly Rooms and the 'must visit' Fashion Museum on Saville Row in Bath. It is decorated in authentic 1930s and 40s style with dainty china tea sets, embroidered tablecloths, bevelled mirrors and wartime posters. The exterior curved frontage with leaded windows is attractive and enticing.

The Regal Restaurant & Bar

33 St Aldgate Street, Kings Square, Gloucester GL1 1RP
01452 332344 Built 1939 www.jdwetherspoon.co.uk

This J.D. Wetherspoons restaurant and bar, is located in the old Regal Cinema. The exterior is typical Art Deco architecture for cinemas of the time and has a warm stone façade. The original large Regal sign is still in situ and the glass doors and windows on the frontage are just like they were when the Regal was still a cinema. This is a great place to enjoy lunch or a drink whilst remembering all the stars of the silver screen.

The Daffodil

18-20 Suffolk Parade, Cheltenham,
Gloucestershire GL50 2EA
01242 700055 www.thedaffodile.com Built 1922

This restaurant is housed in Cheltenham's first purpose built picture palace, an original 1920s cinema. This venue captures the entire Art Deco scene. It has the Circle Bar which occupies the mezzanine circle balcony which overlooks the restaurant and open kitchen below. The furnishings are all in deco style with grand leather tub chairs and original deco light fittings. Frequent live Jazz and music events enhance the atmosphere even further. This really is a top notch restaurant and venue.

Bill's Café and Restaurant

140-142 The Parade, Leamington Spa, Warwickshire CV32 LAG
01926 431203 www.bills-website.co.uk

Restored back to its former Art Deco glory days, Bill's Leamington Spa restaurant is a real beau
With exposed pillars and beams, chandeliers and vintage mirrors, it's particularly beautiful at nig

---

Bovey Castle Hotel Restaurant

Dartmoor National Park, North Bovey, Devon TQ13 8RE 01647 445000

This luxurious hotel has the glorious Great Western Restaurant. It is, in the words of the hotel, 'relaxed and comfortable, yet upscale and classy'. It certainly is this as the décor and furnishings recall all the glamour of the bygone era with firm deco influences.

In the other public areas you will also find many references to the Edwardian era with beautiful wood panelling and tiled floors.

Smith's Brasserie and the Oak Bar are in the contemporary modern style with a throwback to the jazzy 1930s.

Harvester Restaurant

Beacon Quay
Torbay
Torquay
Devon TQ1 2RD

01803 380004

This Harvester eatery is housed in an art deco building with an impressive round glass skylight. The interior is not in the art deco style but exteriorly the adjoining buildings along the quayside fit in well with the deco theme.

SOUTH WEST
THEATRES & CINEMAS

Odeon & UCI Cinema

Union Street, Bristol BS1 2DS Built 1938

This classic Odeon art deco style building opened with Deanna Durbin in 'Mad About Music' much acclaim. The cinema exterior is all that remains of the art deco dream palace as redevelopmen over the years has stripped the original features away. However that said the exterior has a lar; rotunda corner entrance and the façade is covered with cream fiancé tile. It has 3 screens.

Everyman Cinema

44 Whiteladies Road,, Clifton, Bristol BS8 2NH Built 1921

With a mixed history of rises and falls with numerous cinema owners, this early art deco sty cinema still has its original ballroom, which doubled as the luxurious Rendezvous café-restaurai In 2001 it was nearly converted to a gymnasium but fortunately public opinion won and this wa rejected. In January 2015 it was announced that Everyman Media Group would restore and ope the cinema again which is expected the latter part of 2015/16. The building is grade II listed.

Regal Cinema

41 Port Street, Evesham, Gloucestershire WR11 3LD
01386 421007 www.theregal.ac/   Built 1932 Architect Archibald Hurley Robinson

This long running cinema, originally The Regal Super Cinema, operated right up until 2003, afte which its future was uncertain and it remained empty until 2009. After a two million poun investment programme, this magnificent cinema is of the highest quality and the Royal Boxes a an extra special treat. Operated now by the Regal cinema group it also has a coffee shop and wir bar. It is a grade II listed building.

Royal Cinema

Royal Square, St Ives, Cornwall TR26 2ND
736 796843

This is part of the Merlin chain of cinemas.
Merlin rescued this ailing 1930s building in the
late 1990s. It has three screens and is painted
in the blue and red Merlin colours. Originally
it would have been white but it does look
rather fetching in its new colours.

Savoy Cinema

Causewayhead, Penzance, Cornwall TR18 2SN
736 363330 www.merlincinemas.co.uk Built 1912

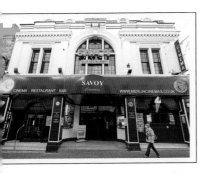

The Savoy cinema is part of the Merlin Cinema group who have renovated and restored this historic
cinema. It has been fully modernised with new 3D digital technology and three screens. It has a
pizza take-away and a stylish 1 bar and restaurant. It still retains it original auditorium architecture
of curved ceiling and original façade now in the Merlin colours.

Regal Cinema & Theatre

Fore Street, Redruth, Cornwall TR15 2AZ
01209 216275 Built 1935 Architect William Henry Watkins

The Regal was acquired in 1998 by the Merlin empire and has been sympathetically renovated and updated. The frontage is back to its 1935 glory. The exterior has a slender fin tower with art deco script in neon lighting. The refurbishment of this art deco town centre landmark has resulted five modern cinema auditoria and a remodelled 650 seat cinema/live theatre within the existing original building, which hosts quality entertainment throughout the year.

Facilities also include a restaurant and bar and three of the auditoria have individual armchairs and sofas, making the evening extra indulgent.

Embassy Cinema

134 High Street, Ilfracombe, Devon EX34 9EZ 01271 862323

This cinema was purchased by the Merlin empire in 2009 and has been fully refurbished. Inside, original plasterwork can be found and the exterior of the building has unchanged other than some new paintwork and signage.

ivoli Cinema

Fore Street, Tiverton, Devon EX16 6LD 01884 255554 www.merlincinemas.co.uk Built 1932

he future of this delightful cinema has been in the balance for many years and even had the backing
Dame Helen Mirren to highlight the importance of saving our heritage. Fortunately the Merlin
npire stepped in to save it from redevelopment. A happy ending for Devonians to enjoy for
cades to come!

Vellesley Cinema

) Mantle Street, Wellington South, Somerset TA21 8AU
823 666668 www.wellesleycinema.co.uk
uilt 1937 Architect Edward de Wilde

his cinema is in the traditional Art Deco style of that
eriod, the large undivided auditorium seats 375 people on
vo levels, 230 in the stalls and 145 upstairs in the circle
ea. Improvements have been carried out over the years
ith modernisation of the equipment. It has a kiosk in the
yer and a licensed bar service.

deon Cinema

dwell Street, Exeter EX4 6PL
871 224 4007 www.odeon.co.uk Built 1939 Architect Harry H Weedon

he exterior of the Odeon is the classic Art Deco design which is unmistakable. The cinema has 4
reens and has been fully modernised. Inside, the original art deco fixtures and fittings have mainly
gone but the building itself is a stand alone monument to Art Deco.

SCOTT CINEMAS

Scott Cinemas

Boutport Street, Barnstaple , Devon EX31 1SR

01271 370022 www.scottcinemas.co.uk Built 1931 Architect W H Watkins

This cinema originally opened as The Gaumont Palace, and like most cinemas at that time had single screen and seated over 1100 guests. The interior was breathtaking with an elaborate 3 co illuminated proscenium surround and cove in the ceiling. It had sunburst effects over the doorwa silk panelling on the side walls with a green cloister-tiled front elevation. The main staircase a upper foyer and bar area still fortunately retain many original, and some restored features. Scre I still impresses by its sheer size and scale.

Two cinemas were constructed under the rear balcony, with a fourth cinema added in the form front stalls, with seating in a stadium configuration. Unlike most conversions of older buildings, ca was taken to ensure complete symmetry in the design, ensuring perfect sightlines. A Cafe Bar housed in the upper foyer and all screens are licensed.

Penel Orlieu, Bridgwater, Somerset EN TA6 3PH
0871 230 3200 www.scottcinemas.co.uk Built 1936 Architect Thomas Cecil Howitt

This former Odeon cinema was designed by Thomas Howitt who was responsible for a numb of other cinemas in the Odeon chain (Clacton, Warley and Weston-Super-Mare). All show h trademark features of a square tower with a projecting supported flat slab roof and cylindric columns.

Broad Street, Lyme Regis, Dorset DT7 3JB 0871 230 3200 Built 1937 Architect W H Watkins

This cinema, formally a Regent, is part of the Scott chain and has a delightful interior. It is designe in art deco streamlined style. Originally it had a 'Hollophane' lighting system, which was whe motorised dimmers slowly changed and mixed red, blue and green lights which were hidden o of view of the audience in troughs. This bathed the whole auditorium including the wave/clo proscenium surround in delicate coloured light.

oxy Community Cinema

High Street, Axbridge, Somerset BS26 2AF 07725051523 www.axbidgeroxy.org.uk

etic licence again has prevailed as The Roxy a little gem of a cinema, created for fun with uch love by local volunteers in 2007.

s design was inspired by art nouveau, art eco and mid century modern interiors. It fers a mixed programme throughout the ear which includes live music, stand up omedy, film screenings, and is available for rties and meetings.

Curzon Community Cinema

46 Old Church Rd, Clevedon, North Somerset BS21 6NN 01275 871000 www.curzon.org.uk

This cinema dates from 1922 and was established on the site of an earlier 1912 cinema. It marvellous as not only does it show the latest movies it also shows the classics and along with museum and educational facilities for the nippers, it is a wonderful adventure once you enter th doors. You can even try your hand at the famous Christie organ for a reasonable pre booked fe

Odeon Cinema

Walliscote Road, Weston-super-Mare, Somerset BS23 1UW
0871 224 4007 www.odeon.co.uk Built 1935 Architect Thomas Cecil Howitt

This imposing building is one of the finest that was constructed for the Odeon cinema chain. The façade of the building is covered in biscuit coloured faience, apart from the shop areas on both sides which are clad in black glass vitrolite panels. The basket weave pattern faience encompasses three horizontal bands of green it is

absolutely stunning. It also still has the origin Compton organ and is a grade II listed property.

©Western Daily Press

Babbacombe Theatre

Babbacombe Downs Road, Torquay, Devon TQ1 3LU
01803 328385 www.babacombe-theatre.com Built 1939

Built in the Art Deco box style the Babbacombe Concert Hall and Theatre was built on the site of the old bandstand and retained its height the same so that no properties nearby would have their view of the bay obstructed. It was commandeered as a lecture hall during the war and ENSA shows replaced the summer entertainment. After the war it soon became a thriving venue with the likes of Norman Vaughan, Bruce Forsythe and the Glen Miller Orchestra. Over the years it has had to campaign and rally support to keep open and fortunately now, it is here to stay.

SOUTH WEST LIDOS

Wiveliscombe Open Air Pool

Wiveliscombe, Taunton, Somerset TA4 2TA
01984 624720
www.wiveypool.net www.wiveliscombe.com
Built 1927 Architect William White

Affectionately known to locals as 'Wivey' pool this heated outdoor pool is run by a dedicated group of volunteers.

Originally the water was supplied from local reservoirs without treatment, but in the 1980s and 90s it was upgraded with some new pumps. In 2002 it underwent further renovations with a new liner and much larger, more efficient pumps installed. This glorious 27 m by 10 m pool is now fortunately preserved and available for us all to enjoy. Hats off to all you hard working vollies! (also in the pipeline are showers and a paddling pool).

Stratford Park Leisure Centre

Stratford Road, Stroud, Gloucestershire GL5 4AF
01453 766771 www.stroud.gov.uk Built 1937 Architect F.S. Cutler

This glorious 50m outdoor swimming pool has lovely Cotswold limestone pavilions either ends of the pool. The pavilions have hipped roofs and terracing. It has the iconic 1930s lido concrete diving board which is 10 m high. These were cast in situ. It curved and has 3 different levels of diving boards. The leisure complex is managed by CCL Leisure on behalf of Stroud District Council, which incorporates a new indoor pool.

Greenbank Swimming Pool

Wilfrid Road, Street, Somerset BA16 0EU
01458 442468 www.greenbankpool.co.uk Built 1937

This 30 metre long and 12 metre wide heated pool was a gift from Alice Clark to the local people. Most of the town's prosperity came from the now famous Clark's shoemakers who had their headquarters in Street and still do to this day. It also has a semi circular children's pool.

ymington Seawater Baths

mington, Hampshire SO41 3RU 01590 674865
ww.lymingtonseawaterbaths.org.uk Built 1833 Architect William Barlett

is very large 90 metre by 30 metre unheated sea water swimming pool is chlorinated to prevent
ae growing. It remarkably dates back to 1833 and in 1929 it was improved by the Lymington
th Company. It is now managed by Lymington and Pennington Town Council.

athhurst Swimming Pool

gh Street, Lydney, Gloucestershire GL15 5DY
594 842625 www.bathurstpool.co.uk

is pool, built in 1920, is unheated and measures 41 metres by 17
etres. It was presented to the town by the Bathurst Family. It is now
n by a charitable trust – 'The Friends of Bathurst Pool' who do an
miral job in fundraising and maintaining it.

inksey Pool

nksey Park, Lake Street, Oxford OX1 4RP 01865 467079 / 252826 Built 1934 www.oxford.gov.uk

Hinksey Pool is on the site of the old Oxford
Waterworks which operated from 1854 to
1933. The Council created this outdoor pool
using the filter beds, and the old settlement tank
was cleverly converted into a children's boating
lake. This is one of the largest outdoor pools in
Europe and it has a capacity of 1.5 million litres
of clean and heated water. It is absolutely
wonderful to be able to frolic around in the
parkland with a picnic and enjoy the water.

Ashburton Open Air

wimming Pool, Love Lane, Ashburton, Newton Abbot, Devon TQ13 7FJ
364 652828 Built 1924 www.teignbridge.gov.uk/outdoorpools/ashburton

This heated pool which is 21m by 9m was
originally built as part of a hotel complex (which
is now private accommodation) but was later
taken over by the council as a public pool. It has
showers and a pleasant lawned sunbathing area. It
is run by Teignbridge District Council.

Bude Sea Pool

Summerleaze Beach, Bude, Cornwall Built 1930s www.budeseapool.org

Cornwall is very fortunate as it has a collection of tidal pools which fill up with sea water at every high tide. These trapped pools have gloriously warm water as the sun heats the isolated water. These are popular with families as they are protected from the ocean current and large waves. Chapel Rock pool at Perranporth is one such pool but many other natural occurring tidal pools exist. The most impressive is Bude Sea Pool which is a yearly pilgrimage for mai families.

It is part man made and part carved from the beautiful rocks which surround it. Being 90 metr in length and 45 metres width it provides safe swimming, but please bear in mind it does depei on the tide times. The pool used to be looked after by the council but now it has a dedicati team of volunteers who are trying to preserve it for future generations.

The Friends of Bude Pool (FoBSP) was formed in 2011 when it was uncertain as to whether would be demolished. Like all the hard working and passionate volunteers who are tirelessly savii our very important heritage they always welcome further support.

Friends of Bude Sea Pool

Jubilee Pool

Battery Road, Promenade, Penzance, Cornwall TR18 4AA
01736 369224 www.jubileepool.co.uk Built 1935 Architect F Latham

This grade II listed baths has to be one of the most well known and beautiful lidos in Britain. It is triangular in shape and has a Mediterranean feel to it. It is only re-filled with sea water during the highest spring tides. It has magnificent views across to Mounts Bay. It also has a shallow pool for young children to enjoy. Over the years the pool has faced many a crisis along the way as to its future. Fortunately the awe inspiring 'Friends of Jubilee Pool' have stoically worked alongside Cornwall Council, Carrick Leisure Trust and the successor Tempus Leisure to ensure the future for this most iconic monument to art deco lido design.

hepton Mallet Outdoor Pool

aftgate Avenue, Shepton Mallet, Somerset 01749 342146

his lido was built late in the 1950s and has had a big investment of money to get it back to its ory days over the past 10 years. It has a an inventive way of receiving its heat, of which 40% is rived via special pipes from the nearby Cider Company and its chilling works. The pool is 33 etres long and has a children's play area, changing rooms and relaxing green area.

lorthcroft Leisure Centre & Lido

orthcroftLane, Newbury, Berkshire RG14 1RS
635 31199 www.leisurecentre.com Built 1937 Architect B Sargeant

his heated lido was completely rebuilt in 1937. The original pool on the site dates back to 1870. is long and narrow, 72 metres in length by approx 12 metres wide. There is also a 10 metre ildren's pool and a conservatory overlooking the pool. It has an adjoining modern sports omplex and indoor pools.

inside Lido

oe Road, Plymouth, Devon PL1 3DE
752 261915 www.everyoneactive.com/centre/tinside-lido/ Built 1935 Architect S Wibberley

his Lido is part of a striking complex of buildings which had sadly been badly neglected. After an ormous 4 million pound injection to totally renovate and stabilise the foundations to the bedrock low and refurbish it back to its glory days, it reopened it doors once again in 2003. The main ilding is made of reinforced concrete; it has a flat roof and a glorious sun terrace. The iconic

semi-circular pool and sweeping colonnades above the structure are dramatic and visually anch
this mesmerising piece of art deco design. This has to be at the top of anyone's wish list of Lid
to visit. This grade II listed lido is run by the City of Plymouth Council.

Hilsea Lido

London Road, Hilsea, Portsmouth, Hampshire PO2 9RP
023 9266 2440 Built 1935 Architect Joseph Parkin

This unheated pool which measures 67m leng
by 18m width is set amongst a large and pleasa
park. It has a children's paddling pool and café.
reopened in 2014 after restoration and is happ
here to stay with thanks to 'Hilsea Lido Pool f
the People Trust', a registered charity, which sav
this wonderful site for us all to enjoy.

SOUTH WEST PLACES OF INTEREST

House of Fraser

Old Christchurch Road, Bournemouth, Dorset BH1 2AA

This building is sheer deco exuberance at its best. It has a warm cream stone exterior which is decorated with sunburst designs acting as dividers between the windows. These appear to have a blue hue and can also be seen on the towers. Be sure to go in the building and have a look at the fine metalwork on the lift frame. Also remember that most of the department stores have café and restaurants so you can experience these buildings from the inside and the café here has lovely views.

Beales Department Store

Old Christchurh Road, Bournemouth, Dorset BH1 1LJ
01202 552022 www.beales.co.uk

Beales Department store is a historic family run business and is a delightful place to spend a couple of hours taking lunch in the restaurant and wandering around the different sections and departments. Its history dates back to 1881 in Bournemouth and during the Second World War the original building was demolished after suffering from the Luftwaffe. It was then moved to temporary accommodation before a new store was built on the same site and in the curvilinear art deco style in 1960.

Beales department store today
and the store before it was bombed in 1943

Bournemouth Pavilion

Westover Road, Bournemouth, Dorset BH1 2BU
www.bournemouthpavilion.co.uk Built 1929 Architects Home & Knight

This building is often referred to as an art deco jewel in Bournemouth's crown by locals and alike. The Pavilion Theatre and Ballroom are open all year, holding some wonderful dances and events. They both retain the elegant styling and splendour of a bygone age.

The Pavilion's main auditorium was not called a theatre, but a Concert Hall. It was soon realised that it had shortcomings in presenting staged productions. Hence, in 1933 the stage was enlarged, both in dep and height, and it was reopened as a theatre in 1934. Over the year further alterations have be undertaken, including the addition of two storeys to either side of the main entrance in the early 195 It is grade II listed and owned and managed by Bournemouth Borough Council.

Bournemouth Daily Echo Building

Richmond Hill, Bournemouth, Dorset BH2 6HH
01202 554601 Built 1935 Architect Seal & Hardy

This building was once a busy newspaper, but with the computer age it gradually moved its printi and main offices elsewhere and now only occupies the upper levels for office space alone.

The original construction used over half a million bricks along with a massive amount of whi monks park bath stone and purbeck stone. It has a magnificent central stairwell, and the downstai of the building was, until recently, a restaurant. The building is grade II listed, and hopefully it w be put to good use soon.

Coleton Fishacre

Brownstone Road, Kingswear, Devon TQ6 0EQ
01803 842382 Built 1923 Architect Oswald Milne www.nationaltrust.org.uk

This has to be my favourite of all National Trust properties, designed in the 1920s for Rupert and Lady Dorothy D'Oyle Carte. The house contains distinctive Art Deco decoration, furniture, fixtures and fittings throughout. The light, stylish rooms evoke the sense of the era with music echoing the family's Gilbert and Sullivan connections. You just need to bring your luggage and it has the feel that you could instantly move in and make it your family home.

The exterior of the property is Arts and Crafts to echo the nature of the landscape it sits in.

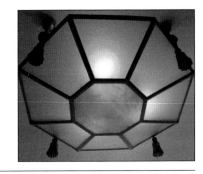

reenway House

reenway Road, Galmpton, Near Brixham, Devon TQ5 0ES 01803 842382 www.ntsouthwest.co.uk

etic licence has allowed me to add Agatha hristie's holiday home, now owned by the ational Trust. This property and grounds ally are evocative of the 1930s and her esence is overwhelming in the property d outbuildings. Even though it is scribed as being left in a 1950s era I feel leans more to the latter as her large llection of ephemera and memorabilia is at of a much earlier period. Dean Man's lly was filmed here in 2013 and you half pect Poirot or Ariadne Oliver to saunter out from behind a camellia bush in the extensive gardens. If you play the piano you are actively encouraged to tickle the ivories of the Steinway in the Morning room but it is kindly requested 'no chopsticks'!

The Lodge house at the entrance to the driveway is now a National Trust holiday let as is the apartment on the 3rd floor of Greenway House which sleeps 8 people.

Photograph of actor David Suchet as Poirot and Zoe Wannamaker as Ariadne Oliver.

©NT

a Belle Art Deco & Interiors

Fore Street, Redruth, Cornwall TR15 2AF
209 216228 www.labelle-artdecoandantiques.co.uk
his specialist Art Deco shop has an abundance of stylish furniture d high quality original items relating to the 1920s and 30s.

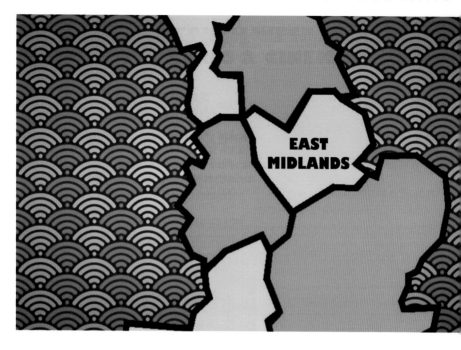

EAST MIDLANDS

Accommodation	149
Restaurants, Bars & Cafes	151
Theatres & Cinemas	155
Lidos	158
Places of Interest	160

EAST MIDLANDS ACCOMMODATION

Derby Conference Centre and Hotel

London Road, Alvaston, Derby DE24 8UX

01332 861842   www.thederbyconferencecentre.com   Built 1938   Architect William H. Hamlyn

This fabulous building was designed by the London Midland and Scottish Railway's principal architect as a training college for railway staff, which also provided them with accommodation. In 1991 a conference suite was built allowing the property to offer further services. It was in 2007 that the company RTC Group fully renovated and restored the hotel, with its sunken lounge, bar, restaurant and conference suites which have been returned to their former glory. The 50 bedrooms are decorated in modern style. It is a Grade II listed property which has a commanding exterior in typical Deco architecture design. The art deco feature flooring and staircase are wonderful.

52 & 54 Inge Street

Birmingham, West Midlands   0344 335 1287   www.nationaltrustholidays.org.uk

These two NT holiday properties, known as 'back to backs' as the properties literally backed on to each other, have kept their 1930s styling with furnishings throughout the three floors. They have art deco style sofas and armchairs along with other fittings and fixtures. They have been adapted for all 'mod cons' and it is particularly nice as you can experience living history in a property which, at the time, would have been vastly overcrowded and the residents worn ragged with working all hours of the day. They have one double bedroom with en-suite shower room and lavatory. The kitchen and dining room are on the ground floor.

Cottage Ref: 018004 & 018005.

Charlotte House Hotel

The Lawns, Union Road, Lincoln LN1 3BJ
01522 541000 www.charlottehouse jpchotelsandleisure.co.uk

Charlotte House Hotel resides directly opposite Lincoln Castle and Cathedral. Surrounded by 8 acres of landscaped gardens, the complex also houses the Sir Joseph Banks tropical conservatory with its extensive collection of exotic plants and water features, and John Dawber gardens.

With 14 unique rooms and suites and a choice of contemporary or traditional to choose from there is something to suit every ones taste. It was originally a hospital but has now been transformed into a luxury hotel with art deco influences echoed in the interior design and fittings.

EAST MIDLANDS RESTAURANTS, BARS & CAFES

ando's

Market Place, Derby, Derbyshire DE1 3AH 01332 371 459 Built 1925 www.nandos.co.uk

teriorly this is a fine example of Art Deco building which was iginally home to the partment store Barlow and ylor and then spending many ars as the Derbyshire Building ciety. To appreciate this large ilding you do need to stand at me distance and across the her side of the road. You can ll see the original Derbyshire ilding Society signage.

lue Peter

ardlow Road, Alvaston, Derby, Derbyshire DE24 0JH 01332 754912 Built 1935

is art deco design pub was one of three identical builds in the 1930s resembling ocean liners as nificant development started in the area at that time. The Blue Pool pub on Stenson Road is w a Tesco Express and the Blue Boy at Wiltshire Road, Chaddesden is a Heron frozen food tlet. They have all kept their marvellous art deco exteriors, but the interiors have all been altered. wever, the Blue Peter is still what it was intended for – a pint or G&T or whatever tickles your cy.

Michael Frith at Bennetts Brasserie

8 Iron Gate, Derby
Derbyshire DE1 3AL
01332 344261 www.michaelfrithcuisine.co.uk

This delightful art deco style brasserie is situated on the balcony at the rear of the Iron Gate store. The art deco furnishings and fine dining is a delightful oasis to come across in this stylish store.

The General Havelock

35 Stanton Road, Ilkeston, Derbyshire DE7 5FW 0155 944 3236

Whilst the owners of this pub, the Rutherford brothers, were renovating it in 2011 they foun many original art deco features including the amazing flooring and tiling in the lavatories. Th decided to invest money to retain and enhance the original history of the pub. You will find traditional 1930s pub with no televisions on the walls, but a fine selection of real ales and a goo old fashioned atmosphere and delicious food without the distraction of loud music and oversiz screens. They have even reinstated the art deco terrace for enjoying that real ale alfresco.

The Test Match Pub

Gordon Square, West Bridgford, Nottingham NG2 5LP 0115 981 1481

This Art Deco building has revolving doors at the front of the pub and an art deco interior. It used to be a hotel and still has that atmosphere. A grand staircase sweeps up in a curve to the upper function room. A dining area set aside like a fine hotel restaurant from that bygone era. It's a Greene King Pub company. It has a traditional hotel bar, art deco in style. The art deco saloon bar is stunning and there are a number of raised areas where bands and singers can perform. It has an original wooden sprung dance floor from 1938. The fine art deco clock on the wall adds to the overall nostalgia trip. It is a grade II listed property.

Bean Caffe

Old Magistrates Building, Full Street, Derby DE1 3AF 01332 742 705 www.beancaffe.co.uk

This café is situated in the grade II listed former Magistrates Court building which is art deco in design. For coffee connoisseurs it caters for all your needs, but for tea lovers it also came up trumps with the 'tea and stickies'.

In other parts of the building there is a beautiful sweeping art deco staircase and ornamentation on the walls. If you get the chance to wander around the other areas it is well worth it.

Cosmo Restaurant

London Road, Derby DE1 2PA
01332 295300 www.cosmo-restaurants.co.uk Built 1934 Architect W E Trent

Originally opened as the Gaumont Palace cinema this art deco designed building has changed hand on many occasions. Inside it is light and airy and serves Pan-Asian cooking.

EAST MIDLANDS THEATRES & CINEMAS

Pictureville Cinema

National Media Museum, Bradford, West Yorkshire BD1 1NQ
0371 902 5756   www.nationalmediamuseum.org.uk

The Pictureville cinema which is part of the National Media Museum can show Cinerama on a unique deeply curved and louvered screen. It was in 1952 that Cinerama was created to allow the audience to be fully immersed in the ultra wide film format.

It may not be of the deco period but it is very nostalgic and well worth a visit as there are only three public venues like this that still exist in the world. The museum also follows the full history of cinema from the silent movies to the stars of the 1920s and 30s.

Regal Cinema

King Street
Melton Mowbray
Leicestershire LE13 1XA
01664 500642
Built 1933 Architect – Denman & Sons

This cinema comprises a two story block and the auditorium is clad in red brick on one side, it has faience tiles on the King Street frontage, in shades of orange and blue with the base of the frontage clad in light grey. This intricate design makes it one of the most decorative cinemas in Britain.

It was built in the early 1930s and continued to operate as a cinema for many decades. With declining audiences, the cinema was converted to a bingo hall. Later however, it was reconverted to serve as a cinema and continues in that capacity today.

Savoy Cinema

33 Derby Road, Nottingham NG7 1QN 0115 947 2580 Built 1935 Architect Reginald Cooper

This cinema is the last surviving Art Deco pre World War II cinema to be operating in Nottingham. Gracie Fields was the first star to appear here and the first Manager was the nephew of Hollywood star Victor McLaglen who frequently made visits to the cinema when he was seeing his family. Today is independently owned and with the alteration in 1972 to accommodate four screens instead of the single auditorium it has a choice of mainstream movies.

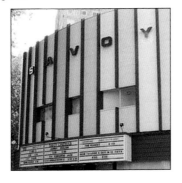

Victor McLagen

Athena Venue

Queen Street, Leicester LE1 1QD
www.athenacb.co.uk Built 1936 Architect Robert Arthur Bullivant

ATHENA

This cinema started life as an Odeon, hence the spectacular design
As Bullivant was from the Harry Weedon Partnership, who was employed by the founder of the Odeon Cinemas, Oscar Deutsch. It operated right up until the 1990s in this guise, when, following a full sympathetic restoration programme, it became a multi purpose venue with a full range of entertainments, conventions, exhibitions and cinema.

EAST MIDLANDS LIDOS

Embassy Outdoor Swimming Pool

Grand Parade, Skegness, Lincolnshire PE25 2UG 01754 610675

During the 1930s the foreshore of Skegness was mapped out with delightful formal gardens, boatin lakes and a swimming baths. The original lido closed in the 1980s and was relocated a short distanc away. It has a large paddling pool and an indoor pool now adjoins the outdoor pool which is 3 metres length. The outside pool is only open during the summer months.

Woodhall Spa Swimming Pool

Jubilee Park, Stixwould Road, Woodhall Spa, Lincolnshire LN10 6QH
01526 353478

This outside lido pool is nicely situated in the Jubilee Park and is amongst tennis courts, a cricket ground and bowling greens. It is heated and measures 33 metres by 13 metres. It is also near the 1922 Kinema in the Wood.

Bourne Outdoor Swimming Pool

Abbey Lawns, Bourne, Lincolnshire PE10 9EP 01778 422063

This lido was formally the Monks fish pond for Bourne Abbey, which after the First World Wa was converted into a swimming bath by enthusiastic local swimmers. In 1932 the pool along wit the Monks garden and the Abbey Lawn were obtained by Bourne United Charities, and modernise with a heating system. The Outdoor Pool Preservation Trust was formed in 1990 to protect th future of this glorious huge 48 metre by 12 metre pool along with a children's paddling pool. It ha indoor changing room facilities a seating area with refreshments.

Hathersage Open Air Heated Swimming Pool

Oddfellows Road, Hathersage, Hope Valley, Derbyshire S32 1DU 01433 650843

This is the only public lido in Derbyshire and is situated opposite the village car park. It has lovely original veranda, surrounded by green lawns and the bandstand. It has new changing faciliti which are in keeping with the lido. It is heated and measures 30 metres by 10 metres. It is genera open from April to September.

Queen's Leisure Centre

Queen Street, Derby Built 1928 Architect Charles Herbert Aslin

This building was originally called Queen Street Baths, and was built to a very high standard, and no expense was spared with the quality of materials. The barrel vaulted ceiling and polished three tiered limestone seating of the Gala pool are certainly worthy of visiting. When the building was designed The Chamber of Commerce insisted that the architect incorporate shops into the main façade to assist in financing the project. Charles Aslins design solution was to relocate the entrance of the pool and incorporate the area known as King's chambers. After renovation and remodelling in 1992 the original baths entrance was reopened as Charles Aslin had intended, and it has two impressive tower-like structures either side.

Mounts Baths

Upper Mounts, Northampton NN1 3DN
01604 837400 Built 1936 Architect Ernest Prestwich www.northampton.gov.uk/mountsbaths

Mounts Baths is an original art deco swimming pool built on the site of a former prison. It has impressive pillars and tiled Turkish hot rooms make this a very exciting place to take an indoors dip.

EAST MIDLANDS
PLACES OF INTEREST

The Natwest Bank

Crompton House, Derwent Street, Derby DE1 2ZG
Built 1932 Architect Naylor Sale & Widdows

This building is a fine example of Art Deco style of the time. It has a decorative mosaic work clo
that has been fully restored.

Austin House

11 Castle Street, Worcester WR1 3AD
Built 1939 Architect John C.S. Soutar

This former car showroom and garage was commissioned by Lord Herbert Austin, the founder of Austin Motors, which then became part of British Leyland and the Rover group.

During its history is has been used by various car companies, a carpet showroom and most recently a furnishings shop. It is now owned by the University of Worcester, who occupy the adjacent site and will convert the Grade II listed building into further teaching areas. It has an impressive art deco clock tower which is a landmark in the city.

Market Place

City Centre, Derby DE1 3AH

The area around the Market Place in Derby city centre is known as the Spot and it has a cluster of art deco features.

As you look around you will see buildings in the curved streamline modern design, often disguised but still evident. It even has impressive public underground art deco style conveniences.

Mount Zion
Millennium City Church

Churchfield Lane, Radford
Nottingham NG7 5GS
Built 1936 Architect Reginald W.G Cooper

This streamlined moderne art deco venue was formerly the Capitol Cinema which operated up until the 1970s. It was then converted into a bingo hall and social club. The exterior as you can see is in need of some TLC. Lets hope it receives this as it is an attractive 20th century work.

The Co-operative Department Store

East Street/Exchange Street, Derby DE1 2DU www.midlands.coop Built 1938-9

This building is on the corner of East Street and Exchange Street and was designed and constructe by the Society's own building department.

There have been many threats to its existence over the years of re-development in the City Centr but fortunately it has survived, complete with its curving sweep of thirties "Streamline Moderne glazing and original metal frames on the upper storeys.

78 Derngate Street

Northampton NN1 1UH 01604 603407 www.78derngate.org.uk

Known as the Charles Rennie Mackintosh house, this was the only house in England designed by him. Originally built in 1916 it has been lovingly and meticulously restored back to how it originally was when he completed it. It is now open to the general public and has many other facilities on site including a delightful café/restaurant. It was the architect's last major commission.

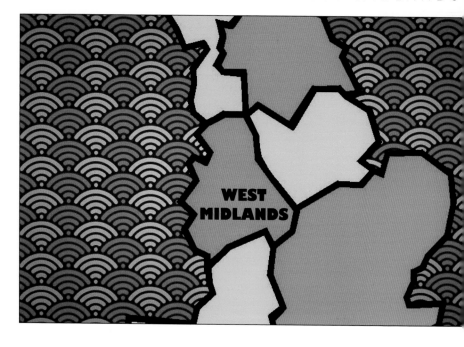

WEST MIDLANDS

Accommodation	165
Restaurants, Bars & Cafes	167
Theatres & Cinemas	170
Lidos	173
Places of Interest	175

WEST MIDLANDS ACCOMODATION

The Edgbaston Hotel

18 Highfield Road, Birmingham B15 3DU
121 454 5212   www.theedgbaston.co.uk

Despite being built in 1847 this hotel has a marvellous Art Deco theme throughout. This boutique hotel has 6 bedrooms, with an abundance of black and gold. The furniture in the bedrooms and cocktail bar is all in the Art Deco style.

Holiday Inn, Birmingham Airport

45 Coventry Road, Birmingham B26 3QW
871 423 4876   www.holidayinn.com

This newly built modern hotel could easily have been built in the height of the Deco era, as the architectural style has a main curvilinear tower, and grand entrance foyer with white exterior and neon signage. It has been tastefully decorated inside and when lit up it certainly has that wow factor. It also has a very nice deco style restaurant and bar – The Grill Room and Flight Bar.

Grimscote Manor Hotel

Lichfield Road, Coleshill, Birmingham B46 1LH
1 675 464 222   www.grimscotemanor.co.uk

This delightful small hotel is not art deco in architecture, but the tastefully decorated bedrooms and public areas have been influenced by the period in its interior decor and furnishings. This hint of Deco works very well and adds to the overall ambience of creating that well mannered bygone era.

Mallory Court Hotel

Harbury Lane, Bishops Tachbrook, Leamington Spa, Warwickshire CV33 9QB
01926 330214 www.mallory.co.uk

Situated in the heart of Warwickshire, just outside Royal Leamington Spa and Warwick, Mallory
the perfect retreat from the stresses and strains of life.

A haven of tranquillity surrounded by landscaped gardens, it is located within the picturesqu
countryside on the doorstep to Warwick Castle, Shakespeare's Stratford-upon-Avon and a wealt
of National Trust properties. With
the Cotswolds also within easy
reach, Mallory Court is an ideal
base for exploring this designated
area of natural beauty.

This property has beautiful Art
Deco marble bathrooms in the
Junior suites and master bedrooms.

The other furnishings are
Edwardian influenced and it is a
very elegant property.

This is the bathroom in the
Junior Suite.

WEST MIDLANDS RESTAURANTS, BARS & CAFES

Rooftop Restaurant

Royal Shakespeare Company, Waterside, Stratford-upon-Avon, Warwickshire CV37 6BB
1789 403449   www.rsc-rooftop-restaurant.co.uk

The Rooftop restaurant (within the RSC theatre) and bar have panoramic views of Shakespeare's home town, the River Avon and surrounding countryside. Original 1930s art deco features combine with elegant modern furniture to create an informal yet striking dining space unlike any other in the area.

Centenary Lounge Café

Moor Street Station, Birmingham B4 7UL
121 633 4274   www.centenarylounge.com

This station buffet with its Great Western Railway theme and original art deco fixtures and fittings recaptures the heyday of 1930s travel with elegance, sophistication and glamour. The whole experience is complimented by the period music.

Brown's

1 York Street, Greater Manchester M2 2AW
0161 819 1055   www.browns-restaurant.co.uk   Built 1902   Architect Charles Heathcote

The exterior of the building is a fine example of Edwardian baroque architecture and you will fin art nouveau detailing in the wrought iron work.

The interior is the 'jewel in the crown'. It is absolutely stunning with marble columns and styli furnishings and fittings. Brown's captures the cusp of deco and is an interfusion of artist movements.

e Grill Room

oliday Inn Birmingham Airport, Coventry Road, Birmingham B26 3QW

his art deco style restaurant is very much in keeping with the entrance to this hotel and offers
ne dining. The flight Bar, with its deco style, is a perfect place for a light snack or a nightcap.

WEST MIDLANDS THEATRES & CINEMAS

Regal Cinema

Teme Street, Tenbury Wells, Worcestershire WR15 8AE
01584 811 442 www.regaltenbury.co.uk

The original Victorian fronted building wa given a new foyer and rendered fascia 1936 ready for the cinema to open in 193 The foyer is art deco as are many of th other fixtures and fittings.

In 1977 the scenic murals were repainte under the supervision of a local artist.

Regal Cinema

41 Port Street, Evesham, Worcestershire WR11 3LD
01386 421 007   www.theregal.ac   Built 1932   Architect Archibald Hurley Robinson

The stunning Regal Cinema has rightfully been returned to its former glory. It was fully renovate and refurbished in 2012 and now has a full entertainment programme of cinema and concerts its 3 auditoriums. It is grade II listed and an absolute jewel to visit.

veryman Birmingham Mailbox

6 Wharfside Street, The Mailbox Birmingham B1 1RF
371 906 9060

he Everyman Empire cinemas will always delight you, as when you step inside them it really feels
ke you have walked back to the Golden Age when cinema was the most important social event
millions of people. This one in Birmingham next to the canal will not disappoint.

has 3 screens which have the seating capacity for 96, 91 and 141, and 2 bars, one which is located
the foyer next to screen 1 and the other is located in the lobby of screen 111. The comfy deco
yle seating and memorabilia and fittings will transport you to that toe tapping time.

ust cannot enthuse enough about these cinemas so take a look in your local area to see if one
located near you.

Even the facilities are in keeping!

ajestic Cinema

hitburn Street, Bridgenorth, Shropshire WV16 4OP
ww.reelcinemas.co.uk   01746 761818   Opened 1937

uated in the centre of
is lovely historic market
wn this cinema, operated
the Reel Cinema chain,
s three screens, the
gest with around 330
ats and two smaller ones
ating 80.

e art deco features in
reen one combined with
e comfort and plentiful
g room make it a most
joyable venue.

The Electric Cinema

47-49 Station Street, Birmingham B5 4DY
0121 6437879

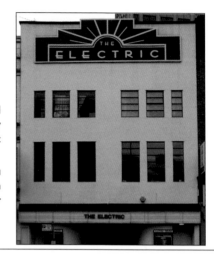

This is one of the UK's oldest working cinemas.

It has sofas, a bar and waiter service. Two digital screens show a mixture of the latest quality mainstream and independent foreign and classic films.

It has standard and luxury seating whereby you can sit on sofas named after stars from the golden age whilst having a waiter service to sip your cocktail or tipple.

Sheer indulgence.

The Regent Theatre

Piccadilly, Stoke-on-Trent, Staffordshire ST1 1A
www.theatresonline.com   Built 1929   Architect William E Trent

The Regent was originally constructed as a cinema and operated as such right up to the end of the 20th century under numerous names and guises. The building had fallen into disrepair and the Regent Trust Fund was set up to oversee the development until the council took over, and in 1999 after considerable renovation and restoration to the central dome and overall building it was reopened by Queen Elizabeth II as a theatre, which hosts a full programme throughout the year.

Empire Cinema

Maney Corner, 62 Birmingham Road,
Sutton Coldfield, West Midlands B72 1QL
0871 471 4714   Built 1936
Architects Harry Weedon & Cecil Clavering

The design of this exuberant cinema is dominated by a central 'fin' which originally was illuminated by the large CINEMA signage. This is adjoined by a two storey block with an attractive sleek tile frontage. To the other side of the fin is the main entrance and curved section of the building.

This is a very fine example of the art deco style and design by these renowned architects.

It has many elements of Art Deco incorporated in the overall design of the property.

WEST MIDLANDS LIDOS

Droitwich Spa Lido

Worcester Road, Worcester WR9 8AA

01905 799342 www.wychavonleisure.co.uk Built 1935 Architect Thomas H. Mawson

This 40 metre salt water swimming pool also has a wet play area, sun terraces and café. The Friends of Droitwich Lido were formed in 2010 to promote and protect the future of this wonderful Lido. It was fully renovated and refurbished in 2006/7 to its former glory after a long fought campaign to save it from demolition. Come rain or shine there is no better way to spend an afternoon.

Courtesy of Wychavon District Council

Sandford Parks Lido

Keynsham Road, Cheltenham, Gloucestershire GL53 7PU

01242 524430 www.sandfordparkslido.org.uk Built 1935

It was in 2006/07 that this site was fully refurbished, once again after a tireless campaign by the Charitable Trust, made up of local people who were passionate about saving their heritage and saving a fun and useful facility for all to benefit from.

It has an Olympic sized main pool, smaller pool, changing facilities, café and all this is within a beautiful 4 acre landscaped area.

Moseley Road Baths

Moseley Road, Birmingham B12 9AN
0121 464 0150   Opened 1907

No, not a lido but worthy of the listing is this remarkable swimming baths as it is only one of three grade II listed swimming pools in the country. (The other two being the privately owned RAC Club in London and The National Sports Centre at Crystal Palace London). It has little changed over the years and many of its original features along with fixtures and fittings remain. It is a Birmingham treasure and if you have the opportunity to visit you really won't be disappointed.

You can seek out other glorious and architecturally important 1920s and 30s swimming pools and I recommend the book Great Lengths by Ian Gordon & Simon Inglis, an English Heritage publication as it has a full account of our swimming pool heritage and facilities of note that are still open to the general public.

WEST MIDLANDS PLACES OF INTEREST

rays of Worcester

2 Ombersley Road, Worcester WR3 7HA
905 754 040 www.graysofworcester.co.uk   Built 1938   Architect Edmund Wilford

is furnishings centre used to be the old Northwick cinema, and you can still see the splendid original chitecture. The exterior of the building has a central feature which holds the stylish vertical name sign, d the distinctive fin on its brick front facade scarcely gives a hint of the remarkable interior, recently stored to its original colour scheme by English Heritage.

eautiful Art Deco plasterwork decorates the walls and ceilings. They are the work of interior designer hn Alexander, his only surviving work in a complete and unaltered form. The designs are of over-life-ze mythical figures, three on each side, and a marvellous example of an Art Deco style staircase.

he stunning relief plasterwork has to be seen to be believed. There are many other decorative features ound the interior of the building, as well as numerous original 1930s light fittings.

Mecca Bingo

ettlehouse Road, Kingstanding, Birmingham
121 354 2551   1935   Architects Harry Weedon & Cecil Clavering

his majestic building, once a glorious Odeon cinema, is now a bingo hall. You can still enjoy the ree magnificent fins and sweeping lines which retain their allure. Well worth a walk around and game of bingo to enjoy the interior which still has some original features.

Barber Institute of Fine Arts

University of Birmingham, Birmingham B15 2TS
0121 414 7333   www.barber.co.uk   Built 1939   Architect R. Atkinson

This purpose built premises which is part of the campus of the University is an art gallery and concert hall. It features a very fine selection of works from the 13th – 20th century. It has a regular programme of concerts and new exhibitions.

Co-operative Supermarket

Wavertree, Church Road North, Liverpool L15 6TE
Built 1939   Architect: Alfred Ernest Shennan

Originally this was the Abbey Cinema with a striking frontage which was strip lit which accentuate the brick battlements. It was in 1979 that it finally and sadly closed. Since then various supermarke have operated from the building. The glorious exterior is all that is left of this iconic building.

pton House and Gardens

ear Banbury, Warwickshire OX15 6HT
295 670 266   www.nationaltrust.org.uk

is NT property has the most amazing original red and silver art deco bathroom which belonged to
dy Bearsted. It was remodelled in 1927-29 and is red and black, with silver aluminium leaf decoration.

ymphony Hall Birmingham

oad Street, Birmingham B1 2EA
21 780 3333   www.thsh.co.uk

is large concert hall venue which was opened in 1991 has an art deco inspired auditorium. It has
any events throughout the year and beautifully transports you back to the heyday of 1930s style.

Athena Entertainment & Conference Venue

Queen Street, Leicester LE1 1QD
0844 847 2474   www.athenalive.co.uk   Built 1936   Architect Robert Arthur Bullivant

No mistaking that this extravagant building is a former Odeon Cinema. In its heyday it had on screen and seated over 3000 guests. That gives you some idea of the sheer size of this venu During the 1960s it was subdivided to accommodate 4 screens. It then operated as a cinema u to the early 90s.

The building has been lovingly restored to its former glory, and retains many of its original art de features and splendour. It has sweeping 1920s architecture and decoration throughout.

The venue is used for weddings, conferences, Glitzy Balls, and can now happily accommodate 15(guests. Also regular entertainment events are staged here throughout the year.

NORTH EAST

Accommodation   180

Restaurants, Bars & Cafes   184

Theatres & Cinemas   186

Lidos   189

Places of Interest   191

NORTH EAST ACCOMODATION

The Haven Beach

Beadnell, Northumberland
www.ownersdirect.co.uk

This stunning Art Deco Holiday home has been extensively renovated and the original Art Deco features have been sympathetically enhanced.

It has 4 bedrooms which sleep 9 with a travel cot. The detached property has a white façade which is streamlined and curved, with cylindrical features and balconies to admire the spectacular sea views, as it is only yards from the beach.

Sandman Signature Hotel

Gallowgate, Newcastle Upon Tyne, Newcastle NE1 4SD
0191 229 2600

This hotel occupies the site of the former regional offices of the Scottish & Newcastle Breweries. It was established here in 1927 but they have been brewing since 1868. Although this is not an Art Deco building, it does retain some interesting modernist features, including the original Terrazzo staircase.

It has contemporary, boutique style accommodation with 175 rooms which are elegant and modern. The hotel also pays homage to the legendary symbol of the five pointed blue star which appears on all the labels of the Brewery's Newcastle Brown Ale by locating an illuminated star high atop the exterior of the building.

The Queen's Hotel

City Square, Leeds, West Yorkshire LS1 1PJ
0113 243 1323

The Queens Hotel is easy to find as it is located conveniently adjacent to the train station and stands proudly over the city square. It has striking Art Deco opulence throughout, and this can be seen in the bedrooms, conference and meeting rooms and the restaurant areas.

The spectacular Queens Ballroom can accommodate up to 500 people, and everything about this hotel just oozes 1930s with the glamour and elegance. The exterior has a Portland stone façade.

adisson Blu Hotel

The Light, The Headrow, Leeds, West Yorkshire LS1 8TL 0113 236 6000

is hotel is set in a grand art deco building in The Light entertainment and retail complex. It has been refully restored to preserve its original Art Deco style, and the variety of contemporary interior design hich ranges from Permanent Blue to Art Deco to Italian all with a twist, combine comfort and style.

ark Hotel

rand Parade, Tynemouth, North Shields NE30 4JQ
91 257406 www.parkhoteltynemouth.co.uk   Opened 1939   Architect J.R. Wallace

he Art Deco style of the hotel has made it a ominent feature of the Tynemouth coastline. is family owned hotel has been sympathetically novated, which included adding further function oms and additional bedrooms. It has 55 en ite deluxe bedrooms, which have raised seating eas and curved Art Deco windows overlooking e coast. The public areas are furnished and corated in a contemporary Art Deco style.

taindrop Lodge Hotel

ne End, Chapletown, Sheffield, South Yorkshire S35 3UH   0114 284 3111

he concept of this hotel is Art Deco throughout. The public areas and 37 bedrooms are tastefully corated in a contemporary style. The executive rooms have spa baths, and they have weekend ampagne breaks. Tom's Bar and the 1806 Brasserie offer a luxurious menu and wine list which is all spired by the 1920's.

he Earl of Doncaster

ennetthorpe, Doncaster, DN2 6AD 01302 361371   1938

cated in this fabulous tel is the impressive d tastefully decorated, rt Deco restaurant, the afé Bar Concerto, with   superb surroundings d stylish Cocktail Bar. his   hotel   never sappoints as the Art eco   features   are erywhere. The rooms are all decorated in contemporary furnishings which blend very well with the st of the hotel.

tuated on the First Floor of the Hotel, is the impressive Art Deco ballroom which can cater for 350 uests and which epitomises all the charm and character of the Hotel. When it is not occupied with eddings or functions, try to take a good look at it, as it is well worth the trouble.

he Earl is conveniently located within walking distance of Doncaster centre and is a mile from the ilway station.

Black Horse Hotel

Grassington, Skipton, North Yorkshire BD23 5AT
01756 752770

This 17th Century Coaching Inn has a lovely 1930s Art Deco bedroom, with original furnitur
The period features in the room are a real delight and the position of the coaching inn on a beautif
cobbled street in the village of Grassington is a throw back in time.

Holiday Inn

A1 Scotch Corner, Darlington DL10 6NR
Built in 1939 01748 850900

This hotel is situated at the famous Scotch corner which takes its name from an old Roman roa
called Scotts Dyke. It is the place where Scottish border farmers used to bring their livestock
market and the most southerly place that farmers travelled to, so it was known as an importai
road junction and still is today as it links Scotland to England and the east coast to the west coas
A hotel has stood on this site since the 16th century so it is fitting to think that now on such
elevated and prominent site an iconic Art Deco building 'rules the roost'.

The Staincliffe Hotel

The Cliff, Seaton Carew, Hartlepool TS25 1AB
01429 852890

With a traditional turreted white exterior this building has a real 1930s feel to it. The Art Dec
feature is the function/ballroom, but the whole hotel just takes one back to an old-fashioned 193C
seaside holiday. The bedrooms are individually designed in traditional style.

Marriot Hotel

Queens Parade, Seaburn, Sunderland SR6 8DB 1936

Overlooking the sand at Seaburn beach is the Marriot Hotel. It has incorporated the former hot
for the main entrance and totally refurbished and renovated this beautiful building. The nev
furnishings and décor are modern contemporary with a hark back to art deco. The hotel has
luxurious suites which have glass rotundas, I fully recommend staying in one of these rooms as
feels so decadent and glamorous to sit in the rotunda and look out to the sea.

Balmaison Hotel

Quayside, Newcastle-Upon-Tyne, Tyne and Wear NE1 3DX
191 245 5000

This modern contemporary style hotel has a stunning Art Deco brasserie. The furnishings and décor are opulent and glamorous and offer delicious wholesome French cooking. The rooms are modern contemporary in design and furnishings.

Dowleth End Guest House

Gunnerside, Low Row, Upper Swaledale, Yorkshire DL11 6PY
1748 886327

Built in 1924 as an Art Deco gentlemen's residence, it has 5 guest bedrooms and is described as an 'Art Deco timepiece' by the owners and this is very true.

Expanse Hotel

North Marine Drive, Bridlington, Yorkshire YO15 2LS
1262 722040   www.expanse.co.uk   Built 1937   Architect E.C. Briggs

This hotel is still owned by the 3rd and 4th generations of the same family. Mr Edmund Cooper Briggs a civil engineer and builder used to bring his wife and 9 children annually on holidays to the area and decided that a modern hotel was needed.

He was a very courageous man to undertake such a venture in eco-nomically troubled times, but his foresight and love of the area drove him on to create a purpose built modern hotel that overlooks the sea and is only a 5 minute drive from the railway station.

The penthouse suite has stunning views and is very spacious. The Marine Bar was built in 1963 and in the late 1990s a function room was added.

As to how the hotel got its name, apparently when Mr Briggs was standing admiring his beautiful building some sightseers asked him what it was to be called, and he demonstrably flung wide his arms and said 'The Expanse of course, what else could it be?'. The symmetrical white and brick balconied exterior of the hotel is unmistakably Art Deco.

NORTH EAST RESTAURANTS, BARS & CAFES

Rendezvous Café

Dukes Walk, Northern Promenade,
Whitley Bay, Tyne & Wear NE26 1TP
0191 252 5548   1930s

This family run café is situated on the promenade and has super views from its large art deco arched windows. Originally opened in the 1930s it really hasn't changed much since then. The philosophy of the owners (the sixth generation to run it) is to preserve it for all to enjoy.

Café Bertorelli

4 Bridge Street, Newbiggin by the Sea,
Northumberland NE64 6EG
01670 857734 1937

Benjamin & Rosie Bertorelli created the building in stages and it was completed in 1937 (it is an amalgamation of a group of cottages and in the art deco style). The ice cream served is still the same recipe which has been handed down the generations. It is said that it was a firm favourite of Queen Victoria, according to Mr Bertorelli. It is a delightful building with food and staff to match.

Francis Tea Room

7 South Street, Scarborough, North York
YO11 2BP   Tel: 01723 350 550
www.francistearooms.wix.com

When visiting Scarborough, you must indulg in afternoon 'tea & stickies' at this quaint te room. It has old fashioned wood panelle private booths where you are made to fe very special. Somehow they always conju up that illicit feeling and the intimacy is ju perfect for a good old 'tête-e-tête'.

The City Vaults Restaurant

3 Hustlergate, Bradford BD1 1RE
1274 739697

This busy city centre pub is an imaginative conversion of a former bank premises opposite the well-known Wool Exchange. Art-deco glass features and wrought ironwork are present throughout. Of particular note is the wrought-iron spiral staircase to the upper drinking area. There are numerous interesting pictures and framed newspaper clippings on the walls.

The Three Pigeons

Sun Fold, Halifax, West Yorkshire HX1 2LX
1422 347001

This unassuming hostelry has five rooms which are simply and individually furnished and have an element of bygone years. The 'jewel in the crown' is main entrance, corridor bar and sitting areas which are all original art deco in design. It has beautiful tiled flooring, wooden wall panelling and cosy alcoves seating. From the outside you could easily be deceived of the surprising interior, as the pub itself dates back to an earlier period.

The Wallow

4 Union Street, Blyth, Northumberland NE24 2DX

This wonderful building has fortunately been saved from obscurity and is now owned by JD Wetherspoons and has been cleverly refurbished and renovated to make the most of the original Art Deco features. It was once a cinema, then an amateur operatics venue before becoming beloved. The resurrection into a glitzy, glamorous and very busy venue is a delight to see.

Malmaison Brasserie

Quayside, Newcastle upon Tyne, Tyne and Wear NE1 3DX
191 245 5000

At the heart of the Malmaison hotel is the smart Chez Mal Brasserie specialising in French and British dishes with an iconic twist. You must also try one of the famous Malchemy cocktails available.

The Ritz

JD Wetherspoons,
143-147 High Street,
Lincoln LN5 7PJ

This Wetherspoons chain has fully embraced the origins of this Art Deco building and has stylishly refurbished it.

It is great to have dinner then go to the Ritz cinema just a few steps away.

NORTH EAST THEATRES & CINEMAS

Tyneside Cinema

10 Pilgrim Street, Newcastle upon Tyne, Tyne and Wear NE1 6QG
0845 217 9909   Built 1937   Architect Dixon Scott

This breathtaking cinema was built by Dixon Scott, who was the great uncle of the film directors Ridley and Tony Scott. It is Grade II listed, and has been lovingly restored to showcase its original mosaic floors, stained glass windows and art deco features. The cinema still shows free vintage newsreel footage during the afternoon. There is also a café/bar and a cabaret style cinema. This really is a treat to visit and once smitten you really will want to come back again.

Harrogate Odeon

East Parade, Harrogate, North Yorkshire HG1 5LB
0871 224 4007   Built 1936   Architects Harry Weedon & W Calder-Robson

This large Odeon cinema is built in the typical Harry Weedon streamlined modern design. It has the tall iconic tower, large curved foyer and asymmetrical walls. After full renovation this proud cinema has been operating for over 80 years and hopefully will be operating for the next 80 or many more.

The Ritz Cinema & Theatre

East Parade, Harrogate, North Yorkshire HG1 5LB
0871 224 4007   Built 1936   Architects Harry Weedon & W Calder-Robson

This cinema lay dormant for over a decade but has now been tenderly brought back to life by The Ritz Team who worked with the local community to rebuild this magnificent building. It is now fully refurbished in beautiful period style and is a joy to visit. The Ritz pub/restaurant is on the ground floor.

Hyde Park Picture House

73 Brudenell Road, Leeds, West Yorkshire LS6 1JD
Opened 1914

This historical little palace is not art deco as such but has been included for its sheer 'staying power' despite all odds. It was one of a very few cinemas opened during the outbreak of WW1, ready for business on 7th November 1914.

the time obviously all the news was dominated by the war but a tiny section announcing the ening of this cinema described it as "the cosiest in Leeds" by the Yorkshire Evening Post. It

anaged to survive through both world rs, the introduction of television during e 1950s, and all the new technology nich was to follow. Proudly, due to its cognised role it has played in our ritage, Leeds City Council saved it from sure in 1989 and now own and run it ong with the Leeds Grand Theatre and era House. When sitting in this cinema iting for the film to start, you can feel e history and sense the people from all e decades who have laughed, cried, nbraced or just escaped temporarily m the rat race of life.

he Regent Cinema

wcomen Terrace, Redcar, Cleveland, TS10 1AU
642 482094   Built 1928

is cinema has an interesting tory. It is housed in what was ce the New Pavilion which s over the entrance of the funct Coatham Pier. Older sidents can remember it as the asshouse' as it was roofed tirely in glass. It must have en a magnificent sight. It ated 800 people and had a ccessful time as a music hall d theatre.

entually like many venues it came derelict and started to cay. Then the Cleveland ema co-operative, ran it as

e Regent cinema for 10 years until they hit on hard times, and it eventually closed.

e a dream come true Mr Bates who had been a member of the former group and used to sell cream in the parlour as a youngster took on the resurrection of this characterful building. It is w a successful independent cinema and the 'piece-de-la-resistance' was when Hollywood came town to film some parts of 'Atonement' and the beach and area was transformed back to the 40s.

you remember Larry Grayson (from the TV show 'The Generation Game') it is said that his nous catchphrases "shut that door" originates from this venue as when a side door had been left en a gust of wind would blow across the stage and he would heartily shout out this rendition. If ly the walls could speak, I would be listening all day to the colourful stories which unfold.

The Showroom Cinema & Café

15 Paternoster Row, Sheffield S1 2BX
Opened 1936

This is a most unusual cinema as it is housed in a converted 1930s Art Deco car showroom, Kennin
car showroom was of impressive proportions and now as an independent cutting edge cinema it c
boast of being one of Europe's largest.
It opened its doors again in 1998 after renovation and has kept true to its origins in style and desig

---

Stephen Joseph Cinema

Westborough, Scarborough, North Yorkshire YO11 1JW   01723 370541
1936 Odeon Cinema

In 1955 theatrical pioneer Stephen Joseph, the son of actress Hermoine Gingold and publish
Michael Joseph, set up the first 'theatre-in-the-round' in Scarborough. In 1957 the playwright Al
Ayckbourn became its acting stage manager. In 1988 Rank Leisure closed the local Odeon ciner
and Ayckbourn, who had spent years looking for a suitable venue, found a permanent home for h
theatre. The cinema/stage seats 165 whilst 'The Round' can accommodate 404. The exterior of t
building is iconic Art Deco style, with strip lighting.

The Playhouse

Bondgate Without, Alnwick, Northumberland NE66 1PQ
01665 510785 Opened 1925

The Playhouse is a multi functional arts
centre, and is home to a theatre and
cinema. The building consists of many
different parts, and has a splendid 260 seat
auditorium. The Theatre itself is situated on
the first floor and there is also new café
which has been completely refurbished
with bar.

It has many elements of Art Deco
incorporated in the overall design of the
property.

NORTH EAST LIDOS

Ilkley Pool and Lido

enton Road, Ilkley, West Yorkshire LS29 0BZ
943 600453   www.ilkley.yorks.com

his impressive pool which is 46m in diameter was built in 1935 and is one of Yorkshire's last open-
r swimming pools. It has a central fountain and slide. The pool also has a lovely Art Deco café
d on a lovely warm day there is nothing better then enjoying the surroundings, with a dip in the
heated pool, then a nice cup of tea to warm you through after! There are good views of the
rrounding moors and a hedge keeps off the worst of the wind.

here is also a heated indoor pool on site, should you not want to brave the outside. The lido and
s surroundings, including the cafe, pavilion and seating area, has now been listed Grade 2.

ngleton Open Air Heated Swimming Pool

gelton, North Yorkshire LA6 3EL
15242 41147   www.ingletonpool.co.uk

his heated 20m by 8m open-air swimming pool in the Yorkshire Dales is managed by the local
ommunity. The pool was dug out and built by local volunteers in 1933. The workers included
triking miners from the New Ingleton Colliery which closed in 1936.

he pool has recently been improved and modernized using major funding from private donations,
he National Lottery and the European Community Fund as well as other smaller grants. The pool
as a beautiful riverside setting and is open from the beginning of the Whitsuntide weekend until
he end of the August Bank Holiday weekend. There are various public swimming sessions daily.

Hathersage Open Air Heated Swimming Pool

Oddfellows Road, Hope Valley, Hathersage, Derbyshire S32 1DO
01433 650843 www.hathersageswimmingpool.co.uk

The beautiful pool is the only public lido open in Derbyshire. It is 30m by 10m and is heated to comfortable 29 degrees. It was first opened in 1936 and it still retains its original veranda, and lawns along with a bandstand, which are all most impressive. Recently it acquired new changing facilities.

The Pool Cafe sits alongside the pool itself and is open all year round, and there is a safe playing field adjacent to the pool where families can have a picnic and play.

If you are travelling in Derbyshire this has to be on the top of the tick list!

NORTH EAST PLACES OF INTEREST

Baltic Centre for Contemporary Art

Gateshead Quay, Shore Road, Newcastle NE8 3BA
Built 1950s Architects Gelder & Kitchen

You cannot fail to miss this building, for its sheer size dominates Gateshead Quay, The building was built as a flour silo in the fifties, but was based upon designs from the late 1930s and has that Art Deco inspired feel. It has a glass elevator, and is spectacular. You can admire it from all around the quay and from the Gateshead Millenium Bridge. It is also conveniently open 7 days a week.

Wills Building

Wills Oval, A1058 on the Coast Road, Newcastle-Upon-Tyne NE7 7RG

In the outer limits of the City is this residential building, which used to be a cigarette factory. It closed in 1986 and the property fell into disrepair and much of the factory was demolished. Fortunately the Art deco front wing still survives and it has been turned into luxury flats. It is not open to the public but well worth a drive past to admire the monumental exterior, which looks like a giant mantle clock.

Co-op Building

Newgate Street, Newcastle, NE1 5RF Built 1930s Architect L.E. Etkins

This interesting six storey high building was still operating as a food hall on the ground floor un 2011. It has been sold by the Co-op to a conglomerate who will open retail and leisure units the ground floors and a 184 roomed Premier Inn Hotel will occupy the upper floors. It is wonder news that this declining building which is spectacular in design, being art deco modern, wit influences of Egypt, is now grade II listed and will once again shine for all to enjoy. The anticipate date of reopening is the end of 2015.

The Central Lofts

Waterloo Street, Newcastle NE1 4DQ

This building was commissioned in the 1920s by the Co-Operative Society as a drapery warehouse. The magnificent steel girder construction with galvanised metal window frames and faced with brick is breathtaking. The utilitarian design is a bold statement but far from being austere and foreboding, the space it commands emits a powerful and graceful management of space.

In 2004 it was renamed from Alfred North House to Central Lofts and converted into commercial and residential properties. The rear is in complete contrast to the front (bright, modern) and it is hard to believe that they are the same building.

Carliol House

Market Street, Newcastle, NE1 6NE
Built 1927 Architect Robert Burns Dick

Originally this building was the headquarters for Nesco, the regions first pioneering priva electricity company. When nationalisation came in 1948 it changed its name to the North Easter Electricity Board, over the years it has changed names many times and the last occupiers we NPower who vacated a few years ago. The building is now only partly occupied. It has an underlyi steel structure, and is faced with Portland stone. It has an unusual curve to the exterior of th building which was innovative at the time for a building of such scale. Not open to the public.

The Sun Pavilion

Cornwall Road, Harrogate, North Yorkshire HG1 2PQ
01423 522588 www.sunpavilion.co.uk Opened 1933

The Sun Pavilion is located in the beautiful Valley Gardens and has been played host to glamorou gatherings since the 1930s. It has a spectacular coloured glass dome, striking architecture with luxurious interior, all reflective of the Art Deco era.

In 1998 after being magnificently restored it was opened by Her Majesty the Queen. It hold corporate and social events throughout the year. It is particularly nice in June as the annual 194(day is held in the Valley Gardens and you can take a look at this beautiful pavilion.

Radio Lincolnshire Building

BC Radio Lincolnshire, Radio Buildings, Newport, Lincoln LN1 3XY
522 511411 Built 1939

This building was formerly the Radion Cinema, which opened its doors at a very inopportune time
World History. It was quickly commandeered for the war effort and did not reopen as a cinema
til 1947, surviving until the 1960s. Now it is home to two retail outlets and Radio Lincoln.

he symmetrical red brick exterior is broken by the white plaster pillars and colonnades, and large
indows.

Former Electricity Board Showrooms

ince's Road, Cleethorpes, Lincolnshire DN35 8AH
uilt 1937   Architect Leonard Pye

his former Electricity board showroom is now a shop, with a dance studio above it, and is a lovely
ght to wallow in. It has many original Art Deco features. The first thing that strikes you is the

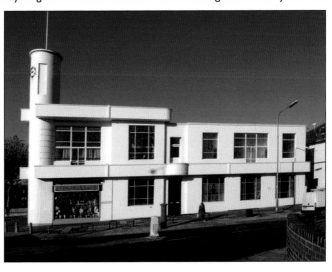

ojecting tower, which
s a parapet balcony on
e upper and lower
vels. It has original
etal window fittings and
iple flame glass motifs,
ong with other art deco
inted glass. The
cessed entrance has an
ik frame and the double
oors have the polished
30s metal bar handles,
eneath which is a
epped frieze.

ortunately, it is grade II
ted, so it will be here
r many more years for
all to enjoy.

The Central Library & Graves Gallery

ader House, Surrey Street, Sheffield, South Yorkshire S1 2LH
pened 1934   Architect W.G. Davies

his building which is influenced by the Art Deco Style was partly funded by John George Graves
866-1945) who was a generous man to the City. He came by his wealth by establishing one of
e country's first mail order companies. With his money he bequested a Library and Art Gallery
vhich is on the 3rd floor of the building). At its time it was a revolutionary building, as it had
visible panel heating, artificial ventilation, along with five different lifts. It even boasted having
ectric clocks.

has a fine art deco façade, which is quite difficult to view fully from outside, as it fronts onto a
rrow street. The plans to build a square with other impressive buildings never came to fruition
ter the Second World War.

West Hartlepool Bus Station & Clock Tower

Seaton Carew, Hartlepool

Seaton Carew is a small seaside resort and it is situated within the Borough of Hartlepool. Along the Victorian promenade you are in for a pleasant surprise as the bus station and clock tower have been fully restored to their former Art Deco glory and are joy to look at and travel to and from.

The Chapel

Durham University, College of St. Hild & St. Bede, Durham DH1 1SZ
0191 334 8300

The University has a rare example of art deco architecture with its College Chapel. It was built 1939 to celebrate the centenary of the College of the Venerable Bede and became a listed buildin in 2007. It is vast in size and can seat over 200 people.

The Chapel is used prayer daily by the residents of the college. If you are fortunate enough attend one of the concerts held in this chapel be sure to enjoy the phenomenal acoustics whi the architecture enhances. The Chapel is licensed for weddings.

Hartlepool's Maritime Heritage

Jackson Dock, Maritime Avenue, Hartlepool TS24 0XZ

You can step back in time as you board the restored P.S.S. Wingfield Castle paddle steamer, whi was a former passenger ferry launched in 1934 in Hartlepool by William Gray & Co. She was bu for the London and North Eastern Railway Company (LNER) and operated between Hull and Ne Holland ferrying passengers. She is 63.3 m in length and weighs 550 tonnes. In her day she cou maintain an operating speed of 12 knots, powered by a steam engine.

You can tour the ship including the bridge and the boiler room. A pleasant coffee shop is on boar She is the largest exhibit at the Museum and admission is free! What could be better then sippi coffee and day-dreaming about the many faces and stories of people who have graced her deck

NORTH WEST

Accommodation	196
Restaurants, Bars & Cafes	202
Theatres & Cinemas	204
Lidos	209
Places of Interest	211

NORTH WEST ACCOMODATION

The Midland Hotel

Marine Road West, Morecambe, Lancashire LA4 4BU
01524 424000 www.englishlakes.co.uk
Built 1933 Architect Oliver Hill

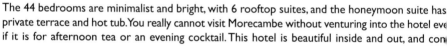

This truly is the 'Queen of Queens' in Art Deco Hotels. Built in streamline modern design it is aesthetically perfect in my eyes. Joyfully we can now all experience this amazing structure which was fully renovated and restored in 2008 after languishing in uncertainty for many years. The stone mural of Odysseus stands proud behind the reception area and Eric Gill's amazing artworks have been restored to their original glory along with Marion Dorn's emblematic mosaic seahorses which adorn the floors and fittings.

It has the Ravilious Rotunda bar which is extravagant and astonishing, with a massive chandelier and all the trappings of deco furnishings and fittings with a modern twist. There is also the spacious Terrace Restaurant, whic is light and airy and has a spectacular sea view.

The 44 bedrooms are minimalist and bright, with 6 rooftop suites, and the honeymoon suite has private terrace and hot tub. You really cannot visit Morecambe without venturing into the hotel eve if it is for afternoon tea or an evening cocktail. This hotel is beautiful inside and out, and con

winter or summer th different seasons shed differe light on the spectacular whi exterior. I cannot think of nicer place to spend a lor weekend. The hotel has als appeared in Agatha Christie serialised novel 'Double Si and featured in Poirot episod on television.

rown Plaza Hotel

eke Boulevard, Liverpool, Merseyside L24 8QD 0151 494 5000
ww.crownplaza.com/liverpool Terminal Built 1939 Architect Edward Bloomfield

is hotel is housed in the old art deco airport terminal building which was originally Speke
rodrome. It is not connected to the Liverpool John Lennon Airport anymore but it is only a
ort drive away. It is grade II listed and was fully renovated and adapted for use as a hotel in 2001.
e hotel from the former airside looks practically the same as it did when it was built in the
30s. It even has preserved aircraft sitting on the apron frontage of the hotel which are marvellous
 see in their original setting. It has the lovely Starways restaurant and the interior design and
nishings are all in keeping with the art deco style and theme.

ere are also two art deco style hangars either side of the terminal converted into a leisure
ntre and business premises.

he Palace Hotel

ace Hotel Manchester, Oxford Street, Manchester M60 7HA   0844 854 2910
ww.palacehotelmanchestercity.co.uk Built 1895 & 1905 Architects: A. Waterhouse & P. Waterhouse

is distinctive grade II listed building is a wealth of design and styles. The Victorian gothic exterior
th its distinctive clock tower has an abundance of pre deco design inside. The influence of the
nerging style can clearly be seen by Paul Waterhouse who took over from his father to complete
e development of buildings two and three which were added a decade later, following the growth
 the original building in 1895.

e elegance, symmetry and opulent surroundings are breathtaking. The 252 bedrooms are nicely
corated in contemporary style, some are with wooden panelling décor whilst the public areas
e the showcase of grandeur. The magnificent cararra marble and bronze staircase which greets

you, screams out for you to 'don' your best vintage outfit and make a grand descent, stalling at every possible moment for full effect!

It is owned by PH Hotels who have invested millions of pounds to keep this gem alive, with receptions area, bar and restaurant you really will not want to step foot outside.

Britannia Adelphi Hotel

Ranelagh Street, Liverpool L3 5UL 0871 222 0029
www.britanniahotels.com   Built 1914   Architect Frank Atkinson

It was in 1912 that Arthur Towle acquired and rebuilt the Adelphi Hotel, on the site of a former hotel. He had a vision to build the most luxurious hotel in all of Europe. This he certainly accomplished. It has many solid marble walls in the bedrooms and bathrooms and marble columns in the public areas. The grand lounges, chandeliers and towering ceilings dazzle. The Sefton suite is a replica of the first class smoking lounge on the tragic Titanic. The great success of the hotel at the time was partly due to its wonderful position, being at the gateway for all the arrivals and departures on the magnificent liners to America. This grand o

Edwardian dame is a forerunner of the Art Deco opulence which was just around the corner. It is well worth upgrading to the larger bedrooms or a suite.

The original marble surround and columned swimming pool transports you back to

knitted swimsuits and bathing caps. Past illustrious guests which have graced these walls included Sir Winston Churchill, Frank Sinatra, President Roosevelt, Laurel & Hardy, Judy Garland and many other famous and infamous celebrities and figures of state.

he Great Victoria Hotel

idge Street, Bradford, Yorkshire BD1 1JX
274 728706 www.victoriabradford.co.uk   Built 1867   Architect Charles Trubshaw

his former railway hotel is Victorian and certainly not from the deco period. However, the
xurious and opulent gold and black bathroom suite in the feature room is very much reminiscent
the decadent and glitzy Hollywood 1930s extravagance. Also Vic & Berties restaurant and bar
njures up that atmosphere with the panelled walls and gentlemans club feel. I half expected to
e 'Jeeves & Bertie Worster' appear any moment. This glorious hotel has hosted and entertained
crème de la crème' of society over its long history and if the walls could talk, I would be listening
evening!

everhulme Hotel

ort Sunlight Village, Wirral, Merseyside CH62 5EZ
51 644 6655 www.leverhulmehotel.co.uk

iilt in 1907, architect William Lever (Lord Leverhulme) employed over 30 architects to assist in
e overall 56 acre project of Port Sunlight Village

iis building was commissioned by Lord Leverhulme and was originally the Port Sunlight Cottage
ospital. Lord Leverhulme was a forward thinking gentleman who had a vision to create an
vironment for his workforce and their families, which provided the best possible care and social
cilities. His business empire was made in soap manufacturing and primarily the marketing of the
oduct, as he was the first entrepreneurial industrialist to adopt modern day marketing tactics,
hereby he branded his products for mass consumption. With his wealth and foresight the
oneering village of Port Sunlight was formed.

illowing renovation and restoration it opened in
)08 as the Leverhulme Hotel. It has 23 stylish
dividually designed and furnished bedrooms which,
e hotel advises, 'reflect the contemporary art deco
ison d'etre of the hotel'. Fifteen bedrooms are
cated in the main house and a further eight are
cated in the Coach House. The beautiful interior
ith large chandeliers and exquisite decoration is
so home to the 'Twenty Eight Miles' bar and
staurant; so called as the main ingredients are
urced within that radius.

North Euston Hotel

The Esplanade, Fleetwood, Lancashire FY7 6BN
01253 876525   www.northeustonhotel.com   Built 1841   Architect Decimus Burton

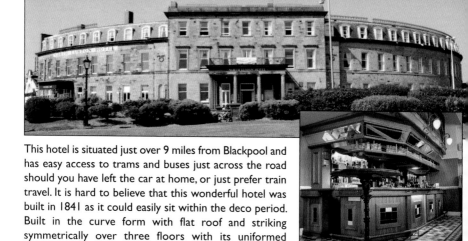

This hotel is situated just over 9 miles from Blackpool and has easy access to trams and buses just across the road should you have left the car at home, or just prefer train travel. It is hard to believe that this wonderful hotel was built in 1841 as it could easily sit within the deco period. Built in the curve form with flat roof and striking symmetrically over three floors with its uniformed windows and doric columned entrance with a warm brick exterior. It has several styles of rooms to meet all budgets, but I particularly like the superior sea view rooms which are spacious and decorated in tradition style. Deco influences can be seen throughout.

The hotel Ballroom is an amazing venue wi curved ceiling and decorated plasterwor The hotel runs many different even throughout the year and many of these a themed for lovers of the bygone era.

Even Queen Victoria has stayed here, on overnight stop, before catching the steam to Scotland, as the rail journey used to stop Fleetwood.

The Corona Hotel

/20 Clifton Drive, South Beach Area, Blackpool, Lancashire FY4 1NX
253 342586 www.thecoronahotel.com Built 1930s

is small and comfortable hotel is set in an original art deco building located a short distance from
e seafront. The interior is decorated with fresh and contemporary styling, whilst the exterior is
its original 1930s architecture.

Gotham Hotel

0 King Street, Manchester, Lancashire M3 4WU
43 357 5555 www.hotelgotham.co.uk
ilt 1928 Architect Edwin Lutyens

is former Midland Bank building which is grade II listed with an
t deco, neoclassical style, was originally designed in 1928 with
nstruction finishing in 1935. It features carvings by local
ulptor John Ashton Floyd, and has been transformed into an
lectic and fascinating hotel. The whole experience of this
easure palace is extraordinary. It is a mixture of gotham, art
co, and vintage – yes, you name it, somehow it is incorporated
side this glorious building and more importantly it works!

has 60 rooms and suites which all incorporate deco designs
d materials. The carpets are in geometric designs and the bathrooms are mostly marble and
eel. The opulence of the fabrics and furnishings compliment the dark wood and leather. The
oney Restaurant would not look out of place in the Great Gatsby movie as the steel tables and
ttoned leathered upholstery with spectacular half moon windows make for a memorable lunch
dinner. The Club Brass bar situated on the 7th floor, which is a members and guests only VIP
cation, oozes of prohibition and 1930s glamour and again as expected is decadently decorated.

NORTH WEST RESTAURANTS, BARS & CAFES

Brucciani's Ice Cream Parlour

217 Marine Road Central, Morecambe, Lancashire LA4 4BU
01524 421386 Opened 1939

This Ice Cream Parlour's art deco design had an influence on the high street shops of the time and if you look around you will see elements of deco incorporated in shop fronts. It is simplistic in design with brown wood and a chrome exterior which has black lacquer base panels to the street. It has the iconic geometric design throughout with porthole lamps above the main doors. The door fittings and even the menus are original. It is like a little time capsule.

Brucciani's Café

91c Fishergate, Preston, Lancashire PR1 2NJ
01772 252409 Opened 1932

This Italian café like its 'sister' in Morecambe is still in the original 1930s Art Deco style. Th exterior has lacquered glass panelling and the interior is atmospheric of times gone by, with o fashioned charm and service.

The Fitzgerald

11 Stevenson Square, Manchester, Lancashire M1 1DB
www.thefitzgerald.co.uk

This 'speakeasy' style bar, conjures up the 1920s prohibition era. The entrance is fairly hidden as is on the side street of the Northern Quarter, whilst the interior has an air of mystery. The lighti is subdued, but resplendent with 1920s chandeliers. The dark but opulent furnishings and delicious tempting cocktails accompanied by the live music on several nights throughout the week, all a up to a decadent night out.

The Stockport Plaza Restaurant

The Plaza, Mersey Square, Stockport SK1 1SP
0161 477 7779

Restored art deco café and restaurant (see the listing in Cinemas & Theatres).

Parks Art Deco Café

West Park Drive, Stanley, Blackpool FY3 9EQ
1253 395191   www.parksartdecocafe.co.uk   Built 1920s   Architect - Mawson

This tucked away café is amidst the glorious grounds of Stanley Park and it overlooks the ornamental Italian Garden. The cafe is constructed from brick with sandstone features and has mahogany doors and steel framed windows. The interior has many original features and the furnishings are all in style with the building. It is such a delightful oasis, with period music playing and traditionally dressed waitresses. Afternoon tea or a celebratory G&T (as it is a licensed café) certainly make a perfect occasion.

Notarianni Brothers Ice Cream Parlour

11 Waterloo Road, South Shore, Blackpool, Lancashire FY4 1AF
1253 34210   www.notarianniicecreamblackpool.co.uk   Established 1928

This family run ice cream business still retains its original art deco counter which is delightful, and still serves the same vanilla ice cream recipe from days gone by, along with delicious old classic sundaes.

The Midland Hotel Restaurant & Bar

Marine Road West, Morecambe, Lancashire LA4 4BU

Please see the accommodation section to find out about the details for the Terrace Restaurant and the Ravilious Rotunda Bar.

Winter Gardens

Marine Road Central, Morecambe, Lancashire LA4 4BU

Recently renovated and restored to its former glory, the beautiful ambient 1920s style French bar is open when the Winter Gardens has film shows and other events.

NORTH WEST THEATRES & CINEMAS

Marine Hall

The Esplanade, Fleetwood, Lancashire FY7 6HF
01253 887693   www.marinehall.co.uk   Built 1935   Architect William Melville

This venue retains the charm and character of its 1930s art deco heritage. Right outside we hav
the stunning Marine Gardens, complete with an outdoor performance space. Why not come alon
and enjoy splashing around with the kids in the fountains or relax, sit back and just take in the viev

It is made up of an L-shaped colonnade in the beautiful Marine Gardens along the Nort
Promenade. The exterior is white Portland cement relieved with faience bands. It has a centra
reinforced concrete dome and the main construction is of brick and reinforced concrete with
structural steel framework to the auditorium. An eclectic range of entertainment is schedule
throughout the year.

Thornton Little Theatre

Fleetwood Road North,
Thornton, Cleveleys,
Lancashire FY5 3SZ
01253 887693

Thornton Little Theatre is a
great little venue in
Lancashire. Proud to be at
the heart of the local
community, they host all
types of events from touring
theatre performances to
plays by local amateur
dramatic companies, live
acoustic gigs and family
friendly shows.

outhport Little Theatre

omenade, Southport, Lancashire PR9 0DZ
ilt 1930 Architect Archer & Gooch

e Floral Hall complex consists of the hall itself and a theatre, added in 1973. This, although closely
ked with the hall, calls for its own entry. The 1930s hall is a flat-roofed brick building on classical
es, presenting a rendered frontage with pairs of columns to the promenade. The proscenium and
ors throughout are in Art Deco style. This impressive multi-purpose building, is a deco delight.

ajestic Theatre

oronation Street, Retford, Nottingham DN22 6DX
ilt 1927 Architect Alfred Thraves

is little art deco theatre was lovingly restored and reopened in 1998 after previously being home
a bingo house and cinema. In the cosy interior between the ends of the circle and the
oscenium are two boxes each side, which are adorned with simple mouldings. The glorious
iling is richly decorated and is wonderfully divided into panels supported by four tall mermaid
ures. It also houses six dressing rooms which are situated over three floors.

he Stockport Plaza Cinema & Variety Theatre

e Plaza, Mersey Square, Stockport, Greater Manchester SK1 1SP
61 477 7779 www.stockportplaza.co.uk Opened 1932 Architect William Thornley

is is one of the finest Art Deco cinemas and theatres that you could possibly find. It has been
vingly restored back to its original condition. In 1932 a joint vision was born to have a cinema
d theatre operating alongside one another in sumptuous surroundings. It has a delightful Café
estaurant which has encapsulated the spirit and atmosphere of the time. The original Compton
heatre Organ with sunburst decorative glass panels, illuminated in various colours, is a joy to see
d hear. The whole experience is thrilling.

Royal Court Theatre

St Johns Shopping Centre, 1 Roe Street, Liverpool, Lancashire L1 1HL
0151 709 4321   www.royalcourtliverpool.co.uk   Built 1938

This Art Deco theatre owes its architectural style to the misfortune of the previous theatre on the site which was razed to the ground by a fire in 1933. The nautical theme which is evident with the interior is appropriate due to Liverpool's seafaring connections. It has an overall capacity for 1186 excited theatre goers. The cabaret style tables in the stalls area can accommodate 290, and it has a delightful Art Deco bar at the far end. The glorious basement lounge has its design based on the Queen Mary Liner. To top this all off, it has magnificent viewing levels in the main auditorium the stalls, the Grand Circle and the Balcony.

Wherever you decide to sit be prepared to be dazzled by this thrilling venue.

Zeffirellis Cinema & Restaurant

Compston Road, Ambleside, Cumbria LA22 9DJ
015394 33845

Zeffirellis is an independent cinema that supports new and emerging talents within the world cinema and the arts. It has 5 'state of the art' screens and a delightful restaurant.
The restaurant décor is in the art deco style and the exterior has contemporary and old architecture, standing side by side which is a visual feast.

Chorley Little Theatre

Dole Lane, Chorley, Lancashire PR7 2RL
01257 264362 Architect William H. Collinson

This wonderful little theatre was originally opened in 1910 as Chorley's first electric cinema. Since 1960 it has been owned and operated by the amateur dramatics group CADOS, who present at least 6 productions per season. Films are also screened in this venue, which clearly is a 'blueprint' with its white façade and architectural style, of the impending art deco movement which was to follow.

Plaza Community Cinema

Crosby Road North, Liverpool, Lancashire L22 0LD
51 474 4076   Opened 1939

ke most cinemas that date back to the 1930s this one is no exception to having 'highs and lows'
er the years. Fortunately for us this glorious art deco cinema has a bright future. In 2000 after
eless fundraising and hard work it became a registered charity and has been saved for the nation
enjoy and it is run entirely by volunteers.

The Palace Cinema

arket Place, Longridge, Lancashire PR3 3RR
772 785600   Built 1860s

is cinema has been reinvented extensively over its long history. Among its many attributes it has
en a music hall, roller skating rink, bingo hall and cinema. It actually started life as a weaving
ed! Following extensive renovations in 1976, it can now be used for live shows and cinema. It
one of the oldest surviving cinemas in the North West of England and regularly showed silent
ovies around 1912. It may not be art deco in style, but flourishes and influences in the design style
n be seen and certainly felt here.

Woolton Picture House

Mason Street, Liverpool, Lancashire L25 5JH
pened 1927   Architect L.A.G. Pritchard

is small family ran cinema has been fully operating since its opening in 1927 with only a few brief
osures. It is privately owned, and offers a welcoming personal service of hospitality. It has a brick
terior with brightly coloured paintwork.

The Epstein Theatre

Hanover House, 85 Hanover Street, Liverpool, Lancashire L1 3DZ
0844 888 4411 Built 1913 Architect W Aubrey Thomas

This theatre started life as the Crane's Music Hall, then Crane's Theatre and eventually the Neptu
The theatre then changed its name in 2012, following a refurbishment, to The Epstein Theatre
memory and honour of the 'Beatles' Manager Brian Epstein, who heavily contributed to the cit
cultural and musical enterprises. The building is neo classical in design but the interior resembl
the splendour of luxury ocean liners of the 1930s. You enter the auditorium via a grand curv
staircase with a dark polished mahogany wood dado and splendid plaster work adorning the wa
The flat panelled ceiling and wood panelled walls in the interior appear to be square. It is t
resemblance to the ocean liners and the geometric panelling which lend itself to the emerging A
Deco era.

Winter Gardens

Marine Road Central, Morcambe, Lancashire LA4 4BU
Built 1878

This venue has had a very colourful history. It started life as a 'Peoples Palace & Aquaria' only to
replaced as a ballroom, then a theatre again. Despite all this, it was in 1934 that a maj
refurbishment went ahead. The interior of the Gardens was modernised with the times and
attracted top acts from all over the country, including Gracie Fields, George Formby, Char
Chester, Edward Elgar and of course Eric Morecambe.

In 1986 The Friends of the Winter Gardens was formed to future protect this historic venue. It h
a full canopied frontage which has been full restored and the project is ongoing. The delight
French design style bar has been restored to its former glory and this atmospheric arena along wi
the allegedly haunted main auditorium are unmissable when visiting Morecambe.

NORTH WEST LIDOS

Crewe Swimming Pool

ag Lane, Crewe, Cheshire CW2 7QX
270 685580 www.everybody.org.uk/csp Opened 1937 Architect – Leonard Reeves

rewe swimming baths are not a lido but had to be included as they are one of a handful of original t deco swimming baths left in Britain and are a thing of great beauty. The outside was quite a velation in Crewe at the time, as the only other buildings in this style were the front facades of nemas. The symmetrical straight lined design of the outer building with a flat roof and exposed ick exterior is in complete contrast with the equally aesthetically pleasing interior. The curved ulted ceiling with ringed viewing seats is a joy to experience.

Nantwich Lido

Wall Lane, Nantwich, Cheshire CW5 5LS
01270 610606 www.everybody.org.uk Opened 1934 Architect – Richard Jones

This marvellous pool is a rarity, as it is the lone surviving outdoor brine pool (highly salted water). It measures 100 ft by 50 ft wide and has a water depth of 3ft to 7ft 6inches. Brine is pumped in the pool from an underground source near to the pool. It is pleasantly heated to 74 degrees Fahrenheit and is usually much warmer, due to the daily sunshine gain. It also has a 1976 addition of an indoor pool. However, the overall appearance, of the lido buildings has not changed since 1934.

Marbury Park Lido

Marbury Park Swimming Club, Marbury, Northwich, Cheshire CW9 6AT
Pool Staff - 07599702903 during opening hours
www.marburypool.org

This lovely pool was built in 1935 in the Marbury Country Park (formerly a country estate owned by the Marbury family, now run by Cheshire County Council) and is set in delightful woodlands. is unheated and has two diving boards, a paddling pool and changing rooms with a small shed. Within the grounds are picnic tables and seating areas.

It is a members club but visitors can pay a daily rate to gain entry. Occasionally in the height the season on busy days it is restricted to members only, so always check prior to attending.

NORTH WEST PLACES OF INTEREST

Mecca Bingo, formerly the Garrick Theatre

ord Street, Southport,
Lancashire PR8 1RR
Built 1932
Architect George Tong

This former theatre operated
until 1963 then was
converted to a bingo hall. It
gained grade II listing in 2007
and perhaps in the future it
may be converted back to it
full glory as a theatre.

AS Antique Galleries

5 Broad Street, Pendleton, Salford, Manchester M6 5BY
161 737 5938 www.artnouveau-artdeco.com

This antique gallery specialises in art deco and art nouveau pieces. Well worth a visit to marvel at
the stunning selection. Do check times and days of opening prior to visiting.

Dock Office

Trafford Road, Salford Quays, Manchester M50 3XB
Built 1927   Architect Harry Fairhurst & Son

This former Dock Office building is grade II listed and is in the process of being converted into 67
apartments. Fortunately the historic fabric of the building is being retained with the off white
concrete exterior and decoration unchanged. The sensitive approach to the restoration and
conversion does include a two storey extension on the top of the roof, to provide private gardens
and roof top terraces. However, the approach of using lightweight glazed materials in the new
structure should complement the solid concrete building and not compete with it. It is a wonderful
building which rightfully should be utilised and cherished.

House of Fraser

98 – 116 Deansgate, Manchester M3 2QG
Built 1939   Architect J.S. Beaumont

Formerly home to Kendals department store this large retail outlet is grade II listed. It was bu[ilt]
in utilitarian Art Deco style with spectacular use of full vertical window corridors from the fir[st]
floor to the roof level.

The Trafford Centre

Dumplington, Greater Manchester M17 8AA
0161 7491717   Opened 1998   Architect Chapman Taylor

I quite wonder what people would have thought if this building had been around in the Deco perio[d]
it certainly would have rivalled all the pavilions at the 1925 World Trade Fair, held in Paris.

What makes this retail and leisure complex stand apart from the rest is that the investors had [a]
different vision from the onset. 'When we first started, the architects said, 'you shouldn't be doi[ng]
all this and giving it all the razzmatazz and showbiz, leave that to the retailers…' So then we put [in]
the paintings, we put in the real gold leaf, we put artefacts everywhere. It is the people's palace.[.']
John Whittaker (Financial Times 11/2/2011)

It is primarily Rococo late Baroque in design but has Art Deco and Egyptian Revival elements ar[e]
influences throughout.

These elements can be seen everywhere in the materials and spectacular decoration. The colo[ur]
design which is in shades of white, pink and gold with ivory, with jade and caramel coloured marb[le]
are dazzling. No expense was spared as the marble alone cost over £5 million. Gold leaf ador[ns]
the columns and there are three enormous domed atria which run along the length of the mall.

The restaurant area is called 'The Orient' and is aptly themed on a 1930s liner. It has over 3[0]
restaurants located on two floors and can give you a taster of what life's like on the ocean wav[es]
without taking a foot off terra firma. It can seat up to 1,600 people!

George's Dock Building

George's Dock Way, Pier Head, Liverpool L3 1DD
151 707 4450   www.merseytunnels.co.uk   Built 1931-34   Architect   Herbert J. Rowse

This monumental building was built as a ventilation shaft and Control Station for the first Mersey tunnel. It now houses offices and the ventilation shaft for the Queensway road tunnel. The central angular obelisk shaft dominates the building. It has a relief of Mercury above the main entrance, which is stylised in modern attire with pilot glasses and a leather hat. Egyptian Revival influences can be found either side of the entrance with two black basalt figures which depict night and day, very apt for this 'open all hours' tunnel. Geometric designs can be found on doors and further reliefs are on the south side.

It really is worth taking the time to walk around the whole perimeter of the building to appreciate the detail and imagery and pay homage at the memorial to those who died in the making of this glorious futuristic tunnel.

Philharmonic Hall

Hope Street, Liverpool, Merseyside L1 9BP
151 709 3789   www.liverpoolphil.com   Built 1939   Architect   Herbert J. Rowse

This marvellous building is home to The Royal Liverpool Philharmonic Orchestra, and throughout the year it stages around 250 events, which include all genres of music, shows, films, and stage works. It was fully renovated in 2014 and is architecturally a magnificent building.

It has a symmetrical frontage with a canopied entrance and semicircular stair turrets either side. The warm beige brick exterior has seven windows above the entrance; these have piers (upright supports) separating them, and they are adorned with carved abstract motifs. You cannot miss the stunning glass door panels by Whistler which depict musical instruments in Art Deco style, truly fabulous.

In the interior of the auditorium you will find delightful sensuous female figures in art deco style which represent the 'musical moods'.

Littlewoods Building

Edge Lane, Liverpool, Lancashire L7 9LH
Built 1938   Architect Gerald de Courcey

Commissioned by Sir John Moores of the Littlewoods Empire (clothing, catalogue, pools) it also housed their printing press and offices. During WW2 it played an important role as millions of National Registration forms, amongst other vital documentation were produced here. Following its closure in 2003 it has sadly lain empty. However, hopefully it will rise again as plans have been submitted to build a 104 bedroomed hotel, offices and business premises.

Assembly Rooms of Jehovah's Witnesses

456 Palatine Road, Manchester M22 4DJ
0161 902 9694   Built 1935   Architects Heenan & Froude

This Grade II listed building was formerly the Forum Cinema. The architects, Heenan & Froude of Worcester, were the same structural engineers who built Blackpool Tower. It lies just over 5 miles south of Manchester City Centre. It is in the typical Deco Cinema style and the white façade with bright red detail is very eye catching.

Marine Road Central

Morecambe, Lancashire LA4 4BU

Take a walk along Marine Road Central and you will be rewarded with 1920s art deco buildings influenced by the discovery of King Tutankhamen's tomb. The former Woolworths store and Hitchens store still impress today as they did 90 years ago.

SCOTLAND

Accommodation	216
Restaurants, Bars & Cafes	222
Theatres & Cinemas	228
Lidos	232
Places of Interest	234

SCOTLAND ACCOMODATION

Grand Central Hotel

Grand Central Hotel 99 Gordon Street Glasgow G1 3SF
0141 240 3700 Opened in 1883 Architect Robert Rowand Anderson

This Historic hotel was opened fours years after the Grand Central Railway station came to Glasgo
It was built in the Queen Ann Style, but has adapted over the years and now has a modern Art Dec
feel to many of the interior public spaces. It has 230 rooms, which includes 3 executive rooms a
13 junior suites, along with an assortment of deluxe and superior rooms. The elegant style of t
restaurant has a 'Gentleman's Club' feel about it: sumptuous velvets mixed with leather upholstere

chairs, and curved recessed seating. The decadent and gigantic bar area with marble columns and marble patterned floor oozes opulence with the domed ceiling suspending an impressive chandelier. The interior decor of the carpets and flooring is all inspired by the Art Deco period. I would just like to say a special thank you to Lesley, who went above and beyond her role to educate and inform me all about this glorious gargantuan Hotel. Her knowledge, kindness and generosity were greatly appreciated.

Beresford Serviced Apartments

460 Sauchiehall Street Glasgow G2 3JW
Architect William Beresford Inglis

This monumental building was opened in 1938 to provide accommodation for those attending t
city's Empire Exhibition. It has ten floors, and dominates the surrounding buildings with its ve
distinctive Streamline Modern exterior. It now consists of serviced holiday apartments (and son
privately owned) which have either one or two bedrooms simply decorated with touches of dec
Please note that various websites offer bookings for these apartments, and the facilities va
considerably in each apartment so please check fully. Currently rooms are available
www.toprooms.com

Aberdeen Northern Hotel

Great Northern Road, Aberdeen AB24 3PS

224 483342 info@aberdeennorthenhotel.com

The Aberdeen Northern Hotel is full of history. It was built in 1939 in Art Deco style and is an -listed building. From the outside it has all the original features and, inside, the ballroom boasts e only violin shaped hall and one of the largest dance floors in Aberdeen. The Northern Hotel s a 3* grading with the Scottish Tourist Board. The hotel has 32 bedrooms and a further 18 edrooms within the serviced apartments next door to the Hotel. The Northern Hotel has the storia Restaurant and Ellingtons Bar Diner, where you can enjoy the surroundings, and hopefully eak a look at the dance floor.

Douglas Hotel

Market Street, Aberdeen AB11 5EL

224 582255 www.aberdeendouglas.com

The first thing that greets you at the Douglas Hotel is the remarkable Art Deco copper frontage nopy. It was originally erected in 1937 but over the years it had corroded. Fortunately due to a ant from the Green Townscape Heritage, it has been fully restored to its former glory. Since the tel was built in 1848 it has seen many alterations and extensions, sadly losing its former Art eco features, but it is a pleasing sight to have this copper panelling on this Grade C listed building, plain view. The hotel itself is contemporary inside, and the bright red and black design of the staurant, and clean simplistic design of the 98 bedrooms does not look out of place. The hotel o has 77 high quality serviced apartments all in the contemporary design.

Blythswood Square Hotel

11 Blythswood Square Glasgow G2 4AD
0141 248 8888 Original building circa 1823

Located in the heart of Glasgow this luxurious hotel has 100 modern, contemporary guest room
including individual suites and a penthouse. The large marble bathrooms are reminiscent of pa
times. From 1910 until 2006 it was the Clubhouse for the Royal Scottish Automobile Club. Duri
the 1920s it then commissioned James Miller to remodel the whole terrace as the cl

headquarters, which was
completed in 1926, which
made for an even more
elegant and comfortable
venue.

The hotel offers a fun and
relaxed atmosphere with
the height of luxury of that
bygone era. Deco touches
can be seen in the panelling,
lighting and public areas.
The restaurant and bar are
decorated in a jazzy feel so
reminiscent of that
decadent era.

The Regent Hotel

Corran Espanade Oban Argyll PA34 5PZ 0843 178 7135

The Regent Hotel is a beautiful art deco building right opposite the pier on the esplanade in Oba
The Hotel, a listed building, is a mix of Victorian and art deco architecture, still with its origin
windows. It has a unique whisky 'Cellar Bar' which is stacked with over 100 different Malt whiski
and authentic memorabilia from times past.

The 83 rooms are decorated simply, and the dining area has kept the furnishings in keeping wi
the period. If the glorious exterior of the building is not a good enough view, it even boasts stunni
and dramatic views over the sea to the Isle of Mull, and you can even watch seaplanes taking off
countless islands.

The Scotsman Hotel

20 North Bridge Edinburgh EH1 1TR 0131 556 5565

This building was originally the newspaper printing house from 1831 until 2001.

Fortunately when it was converted to a hotel, care was taken to keep all the original architectu
features and layout intact, and now consists of 56 rooms and 12 suites. The rooms are all ve
individual. The Editors Suite has original oak-panelled rooms, and in the other rooms origin
features with deco touches are dotted around. The overall feel of the hotel is 1930s luxury, wi
the history of the building coming alive in front of your eyes you can just imagine the hustle a
bustle of years gone by.

he quirky North Bridge Brasserie
as the original reception and
ading rooms. It has stunning
arble pillars and an ornate
alcony. The marble staircase, now
the centre of the hotel remains
ajestic with its stained glass
indow, just like something out of a
ollywood movie.

he Drumossie Hotel

ld Perth Road Inverness IV2 5BE 0844 879 9017

he Art Deco exterior of this hotel which is part of the MacDonald Hotel Group, is very pleasing
ith its typical deco cylindrical architecture and stark white façade. It opened in 2004 following a
omplete refurbishment. It is set in 4 acres of beautiful mature parkland. The interior is tastefully
ecorated in a more traditional Edwardian style. It has 44 deluxe bedrooms and the feature
edrooms have half canopied or four poster beds. The Grill room is warmly decorated in deep reds
nd browns, whilst the lounge is traditional with some wood panelling.

:noc-na-Faire B&B

ack of Keppoch Arisaig Inverness PH39 4NS 01687 450 249   www.cnoc-na-faire.co.uk

his large B&B is in the architectural style of Art Deco. It has the flat roof and cubed white exterior.
he original croft house has been sympathetically extended to give an Art Deco appearance with
Scottish twist. It has 5 double rooms and 1 twin room which are individually named after the
lands.

:leneagles

uchterarder Perthshire PH3 1NF 0800 389 3737

his famous hotel, associated mainly with golfing, should not be overlooked. It opened in 1924 to the
elight of high society and was described by the press of the day as 'A Riviera in the Highlands'. It was
uilt in the style of a French Chateau, but it is the Art Deco styled interior along with the illustrious
eritage that bring it to life. The long list of Lords, Ladies, Princes, Prime Ministers and playwrights who

ocked here between the
terwar years and ever since
rings an air of excitement.

he sumptuous Bar inspired by
ie Jazz age, along with The
trathearn restaurant, which
ecalls the glamour of the hotel's
rt Deco origins, are
tmospheric. It has 232
edrooms including 26 suites, you
an choose from traditional or
iodern interiors.

Balcomie Links Hotel

Balcomie Road, Near St Andrews, Crail, Fife KY10 3TN
01333 450237 www.balcomie.co.uk Built circa 1900s

This purpose built small Art Deco style hotel was constructed by its original German owner. The building is over two stories high with a striking white and blue exterior. The ground floor has the public areas and the 14 bedrooms are located upstairs. It is tastefully decorated in a traditional style

Tigh na Sgiath Hotel

Skye of Curr, Dulnain Bridge, Grantown-on-Spey, Invernesshire PH26 3PA

This small and very comfy Hotel has 8 bedrooms and is mainly decorated in the Edwardian style throughout, along with Art Deco features. It has timber panelling in the public areas and the various chimneypieces are 1930s stone. The ground floor rooms have the timber floor boards laid in geometric patterns with recessed areas carpeted. Particularly nice features are in the small detail such as the window openings which have finialled barley twist timber colonettes. The service bell pushes in most rooms and large green Art Deco bathroom are lovely. The master bedroom on the 1st floor has a stylised Art Deco timber chimneypiece with white and black inlay and brushed steel grate.

The Tin Church Self Catering Property

Argyll, Balvicar By Oban, Isle of Seil PA34 4RD
1852 300010

This Free Church of Scotland, was built in the 1900s and used for this purpose until the 1950s. After falling into disrepair, it has been lovingly restored to self catering accommodation since 2005. The interior is furnished in art deco style, with original pieces sitting alongside contemporary modern. is unique in design and the beauty of the surrounding areas are a spiritual tonic to escape the ustle and bustle of everyday life.

SCOTLAND RESTAURANTS, BARS & CAFÉS

Willow Tea Rooms

217 Sauchiehall Street, Glasgow G2 3EX
0141 332 0521

You cannot visit Glasgow without visiting these Tea Rooms. Charles Rennie Mackintosh was commissioned by the owner Kate Cranston to redesign the building which she acquired in 1901. Mackintosh had 'carte blanch' and remodelled not only the interior but the exterior of the building and designed the cutlery and even the waitresses' dresses!

Today the layout is different as the ground floor accommodates the shop and the Billiard & Smoking Room on the second floor no longer exi
The jewel in the crown is the Room de Luxe, on the second floor the silver and pink interior ar
Mackintosh furniture make it a very special setting to take afternoon tea. I recommend booki

prior to arriving to guarantee a seat in this area, although the first mezzanine seating and eating area is very pleasant. The Scottish whiskey & Sultana tea bread is delicious and my husband gave 10 out of 10 for the Cullen Skink Soup!

The Willow Tea Rooms are also at 97 Buchanan Street, Glasgow G1 3HF telephone 0141 204 524
The tea rooms here are a sympathetic recreation of the White Dining Room and Chinese (Blu
Room, of which Kate Cranston had designed by Mackintosh in her other tea rooms she owned
that time in Glasgow.

Swing Bar

183a Hope Street Glasgow G2 2UL
0141 332 2147

This atmospheric underground venue, with its sultry interior, just encapsulates the Deco age.
unique blend of jazz, dancers, performance acts and contemporary DJs make every night differe
and one to remember. You can book in advance, whereby you pay a little more but are guarantee
to be seated, or just turn up on the night, if you don't mind sipping your cocktail standing. It is ope
from Thursday night through to Saturday. Wednesday and Sunday are nights reserved for priva
hire only.

Variety Bar

01 Sauchiehall Street, Glasgow G2 3LG
141 332 4449

Upon entering the Variety Bar the lowly lit surroundings and Art Deco theme gives it a real sense of character and atmosphere. It has a striking very large fish tank which bubbles away amongst the customers which surprisingly fits very well with the overall setting and design. Very nice to sip a cocktail and people-watch the jostling excited crowd.

Rogano Restaurant

1 Exchange Place, Glasgow G1 3AN
141 248 4055

You really cannot visit Glasgow without experiencing this restaurant. From the attractive but discreet outside you do not know what gem awaits you. Upon entering, the Oyster Bar greets you with boothed seating and Art Deco panelling, wall designs. Fittings and fixtures adorn the floor to ceiling. Pass the Oyster Bar and you are in the main restaurant in the same exquisite design.

The service and food are exemplary. Ask for a seat in a position to view the whole beauty of the restaurant.

Nardini's of Largs

Greenock Road, Largs KA30 8NF
1475 675000 info@nardinis.co.uk

This fully restored Art Deco building which originally opened in 1935 is famous for its ice cream parlour, café, and restaurant. It re-opened in 2008, and has been returned to its full glory with a new contemporary feel. It is a real treat to be able to eat your favourite ice cream or partake in delicious afternoon tea in such delightful surroundings.

The Steps Bar

2 Glassford Street,
Glasgow G1 1UP
141 552 2283

Wood panelled walls and curved bar, red chequer board flooring and leather/vinyl button seating with contemporary red chairs, give this friendly bar an authentic Deco feel in which to enjoy a pint of their best.

Di Maggio's

Royal Exchange Square, Glasgow G1 3AJ
0141 2482111

Whether or not you like Pizza or Pasta, you just have to experience this restaurant. Most seati
is in lovely booths which make it private and intimate. It has an Art Deco interior, which includ
the carpet design, light fittings and wallpaper. The food is very good; I can highly recommend bo
the pizza and pasta.

The Grosvenor Cinema & Café

24 Ashton Lane, Hillhead, Glasgow West End G12 8SJ
0845 166 6002 (cinema) 0845 166 6028 (café)
www.grosvenorcafe.co.uk/cafe Opened 1921 Architects: Gardner & Glen

Despite many major alterations to Glasgow's oldest cinema, it still retains an elegant air of th
bygone time. The scale of the original cinema which seated over 1,300 can still be appreciate
when enjoying the refreshments or dinner in the Grosvenor Café upstairs which has an excelle
view of the original cinema ceiling which is in very good condition after all these years. The sof
and seating area furnishings are in the style of art deco. Special events are organised in the Ca
including cocktail evenings.

Queens Café

515-517 Victoria Road Queens Park Glasgow
0141 423 2409

This may be post Art Deco and of the 1950's but I do so enjoy boothed eateries, or in this ca
ice cream parlours and they do conjure up the Deco period. The battered leather booths hav
many stories to tell and transport you back to another era, whilst enjoying the delicious ice crean
on offer.

The White House Cafe

70 Niddrie Mains Road Edinburgh EH16 4BG
0131 4681934
thewhitehousekitchen.org.uk
Built 1936
Architect William Innes

This beautiful streamlined curved building with a white façade likes to promote its healthy breakfasts and lunches. Fortunately and with a huge sigh of relief it has been given a new life, thanks to grants and a multi-million pound regeneration in the area.

Maybury Casino

5 South Maybury Edinburgh EH12 8NE
31 338 444

The Grosvenor Casino Edinburgh, long known as The Maybury is situated in an original Art Deco building just one mile from Edinburgh Airport. The opulent Charleston Restaurant serves delicious a la carte meals, overlooking the main gaming hall. The Madison Bar is a great place to sip a drink whilst people-watching. When entering these premises you will marvel at the Art Deco interior, the owners have embraced the era with statues, furnishings and glamour and glitz. You will not look out of place in your finest Gatsby outfit.

The Salon Restaurant & Wine Bar

Vinicombe Street Hillhead Glasgow G12 8DE
Opened in 1913 Architect Brand & Lithgow

This now eclectic venue is a listed building and was once home to one of Glasgow's longest running cinemas. During its life as a cinema it underwent refurbishment in 1931 by architect James McKissack who maintained the high standard of interior design. It is a long low building which has dome over the entrance. Seating was provided in stalls and a small circle. The auditorium has a deeply coffered ceiling, with moulded plaster garland decorations on the walls.

1931 it was re-furbished to the plans of architect James McKissack and the seating capacity was reduced to 600. It was an independently operated local cinema and was very popular in the area. After lying empty for a while, it was converted into a restaurant, known as Littlejohn's. On 6th October 2001 it re-opened as the Gong bar/restaurant. It was refurbished in 2007 and re-named 'The Salon' and screens films occasionally.

On 22nd March 1977, Historic Scotland designated the Salon Cinema a Grade B Listed building. This was up-graded to Grade A in June 2008.

Carron Art Deco Restaurant

Cameron Street, Stonehaven, Aberdeen AB39 2HS
01569 760460 www.carron-restaurant.co.uk

The original architectural design created by Colonel H.S. Tawse and Mr Mackie of Messrs Tawse Allan together with internal designer Mr Bowman of Messrs Macdonald & Cresswick of Edinburg

The Carron Art Deco Restaurant is 15 miles south of Aberdeen, and offers diners contempora cuisine in a stylish restaurant that exudes 1930s sophistication. It is rather a unique place as it h a multitude of wonderful features and includes a sunken garden and on nice evenings you can out on the original Art Deco terrace and sip cocktails or coffee. It was built as a Restaurant, a its history includes being requisitioned during WWII by troops for a short time, and traded as restaurant up until 1968. After this date it became rather forlorn and forgotten and was bei used as storage rooms for other shops. During the late 1990s a local businessman bought it a returned it back to its former glory, spending over 1 million pounds, to bring it back to life.

The Art Deco features are based on the historic liner the Queen Mary. The listed building featur hundreds of light bulbs and thousands of tiny glass tiles set within the columns. It has a stunning ft mirror in the main dining area, and there is speculation that it is a rare work by Pablo Picas called the Mystic Lady. The risqué design for its time has never been authenticated, but this adds to the excitement and atmosphere of this truly opulent eatery. Please check with th restaurant prior to attending as it has recently changed ownership and is in a transitional perio

India of Inchinnan

R34 Restaurant & Café, Greenock Road,
Inchinnan PA4 9LH
0141 533 4069 www.r34restaurant.com

This listed building has served several industrial and commercial uses over the years. It started life in its current structural form in 1930 replacing a former airship and aircraft factory on the site, and was known as the India Tyre Factory. The Tyre Factory eventually closed in 1981. The architect was Thomas Wallis, of Wallis, Gilbert & Partners who were also

sponsible for the Hoover Building in Perivale London, so a similarity in style can be seen between
e two, but it does not have the elaborate Egyptian style decoration.

e large striking façade of this Art Deco building has been sympathetically restored, and has been
ught back to life as a restaurant and café. The R34 name of the Restaurant derives from the
ship which was originally constructed on the site and was the first to cross the Atlantic in both
rections during 1919. This classic food restaurant is 15 minutes away from the city centre of
asgow and is situated directly behind Glasgow Airport, and can be seen when landing.

oyal Arch Bar

ook Street, Broughty Ferry, Dundee
382 779741

is splendid quaint and eclectic pub has a lounge that is
corated in Art Deco style with stained glass windows
d ceiling panels depicting the Broughty Ferry landscape.
is is juxtaposed with the authentic and historical
loon Bar with a hand carved solid oak gantry, circa
49. Well worth a visit.

afé St Honoré

North West Thistle Street Lane, Edinburgh EH2 1EA   0131 226 2211

dden along a cobbled lane in Edinburgh's New Town district you will find this charming eatery.
s a mixture of French chic with elegant art deco influences in the form of mosaic floor tiling, glitzy
rrored panels luxurious fittings and fixtures. It serves a large selection of Scottish and French
isine.

SCOTLAND THEATRES & CINEMAS

Glasgow Film Theatre

12 Rose Street, Glasgow G3 6RB
0141 332 6535
Opened 1939
Architect James McKissack

The Glasgow Film Theatre is an independent cinema in Rose Street. It is a listed building and is now a registered charity.

It was originally opened as a cinema and retains the original and restored features. The Cosmo Café which is named after the cinema's mascot when the building opened in 1939 has retained some art deco features. You can enjoy a light bite and refreshments pre show time.

The Grosvenor Cinema & Café

24 Ashton Lane, Hillhead, Glasgow West End G12 8SJ
0845 166 6002 (cinema) 0845 166 6028 (café)
www.grosvenorcinema.co.uk Opened 1921 Architects Gardner & Glen

Despite many major alterations to Glasgow's oldest cinema, it still retains an elegant air of th bygone time. The scale of the original cinema which seated over 1,300 can still be appreciate when enjoying the refreshments or dinner in the Grosvenor Café upstairs which has an excelle view of the original cinema ceiling which is in very good condition after all these years.

Birks Cinema

PO Box 7517, Aberfeldy, Perthshire PH15 2WH
01887 822845 Opened 1939 Built by Strathmore Picture Houses Ltd

Friends of the Birks cinema thankfully rescued this delightful building in 2005 as it had fallen into sorry state, and was probably heading towards demolition. After a hard fought campaign to rai funds to acquire the building and then have it fully restored it opened it doors as a cinema again April 2013, and is now owned and run by The Birks cinema trust. The exterior of the building pretty much the same as it was in 1939, with a gleaming geometric white façade. The interior h been re-designed to accommodate the new community spaces and it is bright and fresh in contemporary style.

Regal Cinema

4-34 North Bridge Street, Bathgate, West Lothian EH48 4PS
01506 630085 Opened 1938 Architects AD Huxton

This marvellous cinema has been a community theatre since 1995. Fortunately the exterior is very much as originally built. The fenestration (arrangement of windows in a building) along with the fine symmetrical Art Deco composition with classical overtones is pure delight. The interior has undergone some changes, to allow the building to be adapted for community use. Despite this there a wealth of original features to enjoy. The entrance foyer space has excellent finely detailed terrazzo flooring, which is a composite material, poured in place or pre-cast, which is used for floor and wall treatments. Original plasterwork adorns the edge of the ceiling and at cornice level.

The upper foyer has original beautiful stained glass windows, and the auditorium has original plasterwork which surrounds the proscenium (area/arch around the stage opening). Also the ceiling still retains its Art Deco detailing.

The large fibrous plasterwork panels on the splay walls above the side exits which were created by John Alexander, caused quite a stir at the time. The images depict a nude chariot rider driving his horse into the sky, and opinion was divided as to whether the theme was acceptable in a public place. It even delayed the cinema's opening by several days. The only other cinema in the UK to retain plasterwork by Alexander is the grade II listed Northwick cinema in Worcester, making this an important historic feature of the cinema.

Dominion Cinema

18 Newbattle Terrace, Edinburgh EH10 ART
0131 447 4771 Opened 1938 Architect Thomas Bowhill Gibson

The Dominion Cinema in Edinburgh's Morningside area is a real gem. Behind its Art Deco frontage and red casts lies a real treat. This well known and much loved cinema makes 'going to the pictures' really enjoyable experience. In the comfort of sofas, recliners and footstools, not to mention refreshments, you can enjoy the latest films. The Dominion is family run and it shows in lots of nice touches, like the photographs lining the corridors which highlights this cinema's history with a star-studded guest list of visitors.

The New Picture House

117 North Street, St Andrews, Fife KY16 9AD
01334 474902 Opened 1931
Architect Gillespie & Scott

This luxurious cinema has a long and narrow auditorium, with a barrel vaulted ceiling. It has two screens (the 2nd being added in 1980). Numerous original decorative features remain, like the embossed letters NPH (for New Picture House) which can be seen in the main auditorium and other paintings. Also the remnants of the original gas lighting system are still in situ. The original one long balcony has been extended to provide additional luxury seating for the main screen.

The cinema has an unusual exterior, as it has a covered area over the pavement to provide shelter in case of inclement weather!

The Hippodrome

10 Hope Street, Bo'ness, West Lothian EH51 0AA
01324 506850 Opened 1912
Architect Matthew Steele

The Hippodrome re-opened its doors to the public in April 2009, recreating the golden age of cinema-going using 21st century technology.

This venue is a rare example of pre-art deco cinema architecture, one of Scotland's oldest purpose built picture houses.

The Hippodrome is owned by the Scottish Historic Buildings Trust, who oversaw the refurbishment which included reinstatement of the 1926 glorious decorative scheme, installation of new seating and original seating restored. The building is leased to Falkirk Council which fitted out the building installing digital and 35mm projectors and a state-of-the art sound system to offer the best cinema experience.

The Playhouse IMAX Cinema

6 Murray Street, Perth PH1 5PJ
01738 623126 Opened in 1933
Architect Alexander Cattanach Jr.

This large 7 screened cinema is now state-of-art showing mainstream new and 3D films. Fortunately the elaborate foyer refurbishment has retained some original art deco features.

Belmont Picture House/Filmhouse

49 Belmont Street, Aberdeen AB10 1JS
01224 343536 www.picturehouse.co.uk Built 1896

Originally this building was built as a trade's hall. It was not until two years later that the first film (yes - surprising to think that back in the late 19th century films were shown!) was viewed here. It was footage of Queen Victoria at Balmoral. Over the next twelve years, films were shown here and in 1910 it became a permanent fixture.

In 1921 it was refurbished and reopened, being re-named the New Kinema. Then in 1935 it was again refurbished and renamed as was the tradition to Belmont Cinema. It closed in 1953 and was used as a warehouse until in September 2000 when life (and funds) was breathed back into it; we once again have the Belmont Filmhouse.

he Picture House

Hall Street, Campbeltown PA28 6BU

586 553657 www.weepictures.co.uk Opened 1913 Architect AV Gardner

ardener's design for the building was quite unlike any other cinema building of the time, which is sed around a series of concentric ovals, the highest and narrowest of which consisted of the ojection box, with a larger oval below that at balcony level, with another curved frontage and yer area below - the curved walls are very noticeable on the exterior facade, and, in another usual touch, were mirrored on the back wall of the auditorium.

here was no foyer to speak of, with doors under a single central ticket box open to the elements, otected only by an open-air balcony above. The cinema was a great success, and in July 1931 the nema closed for 11 days to allow sound equipment to be installed. An additional kiosk building as built next door to provide additional queuing space for customers.

1935, the original architect was brought back to refurbish and modernise the interior. This volved the construction of two small buildings (now known locally as 'the wee houses') on either de of the screen, and the rebuilding of the balcony to improve access from one to two stairwells. aking the most of the small venue, the buildings at either side of the screen are not entirely ecorative; one houses the manager's office, and the other is a storeroom.

iscovery Centre Cinema

he Winter Garden, Victoria Street, Rothesay, Isle of Bute PA20 0AH

his cinema is housed in Rothesay's famous 1924 Winter Garden. It may not be Art Deco in style ut it does represent an amazing structure. It also includes a multi-media exhibition which troduces visitors to the abounding beauty of the Isle. The latest films are shown in a state-of-art 0 seat theatre. Well worth a visit, to enjoy the surroundings.

SCOTLAND LIDOS

Stonehaven Open Air Swimming Pool

Queen Elizabeth Park, Stonehaven AB39 2RD
01569 762134 (01569 763162 pre-season) Opened 1934

During 2014 this huge Olympic sized 50 m long pool celebrated its 80th Birthday. Along the wa
it has faced closure, but due to the inspirational charitable group 'The Friends of Stonehaven Ope
Air Swimming Pool' who work closely with Aberdeenshire Council, it is now preserved for th
nation and the pool operates to the highest standards.

It has clean sea water heated to 29 degrees which is often warmer than the Mediterranean. Yc
can enjoy the sheltered sun terraces, free patio armchairs and sun loungers and café.

Gourock Outdoor Pool

Albert Road, Gourock, Inverclyde PA19 1ND
01475 631561

This pool was originally opened in 1909, when it was tidal and certainly not heated. Heating wa
added in the late 1960s and in 2010 a major refurbishment brough it into the 21st century. No
the water temperature is kept at a constant 29 degrees and is filtered from the River Clyde.

The view from the poolside is out across the Clyde to Loch Long and beyond to the Lock Lomor
and Trossachs National Park, just spectacular, it really doesn't get much better than this. The poc
is open from May to September, come rain or shine.

ew Cumnock

The Castle, New Cumnock, Ayrshire KA18 4AH
7929 096226

though this open air pool was built in the 1960s it has the same feel of a 1930s lido as it was built
the same style. As it was earmarked for closure by East Ayrshire Council, the New Cumnock
community Open-Air Swimming Pool Group was formed in January 2012 to take on the running

the Pool so it continues to
perate and provide locals and
ose from further afield with a
bulous facility they can visit to
vim outdoors.

has a tea room with indoor and
utdoor seating, and changing and
ilet facilities. Future plans are for
w buildings around the poolside
hich include generous changing
oms and modern shower
cilities and a covered seating area.

he Trinkie

The Castle, New Cumnock, Ayrshire KA18 4AH
7929 096226

he Trinkie is a natural sea water pool which is painted yearly. There is a road that runs down to
and on a hot summer's day you will find families having picnics and swimming here. The pool lies
the outskirts of Wick past the old coastguard station.

is outdoor pool cut into
e rocks was the swimming
ol for many a hardy
aithness generation. Still
eaned out each year by
lunteers and painted white
is still a cold dip even in
mmer. Old pictures show
rongs of people swimming
ere in the summer
onths.

exandra Buxton writes
On a hot day, as many as
0 people swim and sun-
the at the Trinkie. Trinkie is the Scottish word for trench: the pool was created about 70 years
o from part of a quarry. It owes its continued existence to the Sutherland family, who as "Friends
the Trinkie" scrub and paint it every year. The swimming season in Scotland is very short," says
n Sutherland, who learnt to swim in the Trinkie. "There are only about 10 weeks when you don't
ss out with hypothermic shock getting in."

SCOTLAND PLACES OF INTEREST

When the Art Deco style of architecture sprung up in Scotland, it was a cause for celebration. The impact of, the British Empire Exhibition of 1938, which was held in Glasgow's Bellahouston Park managed to enthral and entrance millions of visitors who warmed to the sleek new design and inspired architects to follow its design principles.

Luma Lamp Factory (Now Residential Properties)

Shieldhall Road, Glasgow G51 4HE
Opened 1938   Architect Cornelius Armour

This gargantuan building which is even visible from the M8 motorway, boasts a sleek and curving 84ft high glass tower with aesthetically pleasing porthole style windows. The building at the time had a large role to play in spreading the word of this new design style which was to be such important part of our architectural history. It also coincided with the British Empire Exhibition held in Glasgow's Bellahouston Park in 1938.

The building stood out from the Victorian architecture of Glasgow and injected a new wave modernism, north of the border. Prof McKean, professor of Scottish architectural history Dundee University, commented that "…the art deco buildings shook up the architecture industrial Scotland. Suddenly, you had these sleek buildings, that were shiny, or brilliant white, or with dazzling chrome fascias, appearing in soot black streets." The Scotsman Newspaper 20th May 201

In 1996 the building was converted into 43 stylish flats, and has since won an accolade architectural awards.

andleriggs Car Park

Albion Street, Glasgow G1 1LH

is striking, newly built car park has been included, as it
ys great homage to Art Deco design and style. Be sure to
ok at the Deco designs above the entrance, then you will
ed to stand back a distance to enjoy the streamlining on
e stonework and the central element which finishes with
triangular finial at the top.

ecorative brick work is near the roofline, I believe top
arks should be rewarded for creating such a special
ilding out of a car park!

t Andrew's House

egent Road, Edinburgh EH1 3DG
31 244 2636   Built 1934-9   Architect Thomas Tait

is listed building has housed many dignitaries of the Scottish Government as well as the First
inister. It was the largest metal-framed building in Europe in 1939 and the grand scale and mantel
ck design are striking. During its refurbishment the art deco features have been preserved, and
is truly is an outstanding monument to the Modern movement of its time.

Greens Playhouse

106 Nethergate, Dundee, Angus DD1 4EH
Built 1936   Architect: John Fairweather

This former Playhouse is now a Mecca bingo hall, but unfortunately
the entire building was destroyed by fire.

The Bingo company owners realised the importance of the iconic
image of the former building and tried to recreate the look with the
tall tower in Art Deco style.

It is still a focal point in the town, and a whisper to the past glory of
the building.

astle Stuart Clubhouse

verness IV2 7JL
463 796111   Architects: Mark Parsinen & Gil Hanse

golf is your tonic, you will be in for a pleasant surprise
hen the 9th hole greets you !

om 2009 a newly erected Art Deco style clubhouse
igned triumphantly amidst the green. This fabulous all
hite building with turquoise roof was just what
arsinen wanted to build as he envisaged the 1930s style
ubhouse would marry perfectly with the surroundings.
ell worth a visit. No membership needed, and just 5
inutes drive from Inverness airport.

Ascot Cinema (Now Residential Properties)

Anniesland, Glasgow   Built 1939 Architect Charles McNair

This magnificent former Art Deco cinema has been converted into a block of desirable flats, aft
a long history as a cinema and then a bingo hall from 1975. It closed in 1999 and instead of bei
fully demolished the glorious façade has, fortunately been retained during the housing developme
This was the last big suburban cinema to be built in Glasgow.

Rothesay Pavilion

45 Argyle Street, Isle of Bute PA20 0AX
Opened 1938 Architect Rothesay

This iconic Art Deco building has an enviable position at the end of the famous Victorian Esplana
It has magnificent views of Rothesay Bay and across to the Cowal Peninsular. The Pavilion is use
today as it was always intended, to host community events which include everything: variety show
dancing and exhibitions, along with sporting activities and weddings. It has a capacity of 1,000
the main hall with smaller function rooms around.

Girvan Railway Station

Vicarton Street, Girvan, South Ayrshire KA26 9HF

The original railway station was built in 1893 but following a fire in 1946 it was redesigned and bu
in the Art Deco style at the end of the 1940s. It is the only Art Deco railway station in Scotlan
It is rightfully a listed building and is gloriously painted in the burgundy and cream livery of th
former Glasgow & South Western/London, Midland and Scottish Railways. It has two platforms a
is a very busy station which is manned 7 days a week.

The Vogue Bingo Hall

726 Cumbernauld Road, Glasgow G33 2ES
0141 770 4533 Opened 1938
Architect James McKissack

The former Riddrie Cinema is a striking and
exciting building and no expense was spared in its
construction. You are greeted from quite a distance
by its brilliance, as it is a very commanding
landmark. The tiled, white flowing façade is edged
and outlined with black and it has tall windows
above the central entrance canopy, with smaller
windows either side of these. Fortunately the current owners have sympathetically refurbished th
building and still kept intact as many original features, like the radiator covers and much of th
terrazzo flooring. The high ceilings and deco style colouring and furnishings make this a ve
desirable Bingo Hall, well worth a visit.

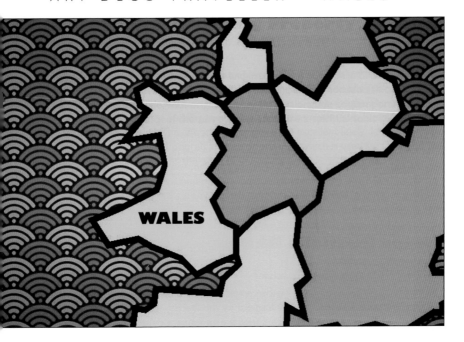

WALES

Accommodation 238

Restaurants, Bars & Cafes 241

Theatres & Cinemas 243

Lidos 245

Places of Interest 246

WALES ACCOMODATION

The Grand Hotel

Ivey Place, High Street, Swansea SA1 1NX
01792 645898 Built 1930s www.thegrandhotelswansea.co.uk

This local landmark hotel is built in stone and sits grandly only minutes away from Swansea railw
station. It underwent a total refurbishment in 2004 and the interior is pleasantly decorated wi
fixtures and fittings in contemporary style. The penthouse suites include hot tubs on the balconie
I particularly like the rooms which incorporate the building's curvature. The restaurant and ba
area have touches of Deco. The exterior of the building is a delight to greet you when disembarkin
after a long journey.

Escape Boutique B&B

Church Walks, Llandudno
01492 877776 www.escapebandb.co.uk

This lovely boutique hotel has nine contemporary and individually styled rooms. My particula
favourite is Room 3 as it is directly inspired by the Deco period. The silver grey, wallpaper an
freestanding bath with matching accessories are an opulent delight. The other rooms are just a
delightfully decorated with brightly coloured designer furnishings and fittings, all creating a spec
space to stay. The building is a Victorian villa.

Quay Hotel & Spa

Deganwy Quay, Deganwy, Conwy LL31 9DJ
01492 564 100 www.quayhotel.co.uk

This hotel and spa has touches of Deco in the foyer with tiled flooring and wood panelling alo
with Deco style light fittings. The rooms are all modern contemporary and some of the furnishin
are in the Deco style. The grill, restaurant and bar areas are modern and very stylish but again evol
a bygone era with the atmosphere and selection of colour and design of the furnishings. Th
exterior of this hotel is of modern wood, steel and concrete construction.

Sunray Guest House

Barmouth, The Quay, Gwynedd,
West Wales LL42 1HB
01341 280985 www.sunrayguesthouse.com

Sunray Guest house is an attractive original Art
Deco house with excellent views of the
harbour and estuary prominently situated
right on the side of the quay and within two
minutes of Barmouths' beaches. All rooms
include en-suite facilities, and are decorated in
fresh modern design.

ouse By The Dyke

hirk, Wrexham
44 335 1287 www.nationaltrustholidays.org.uk

his 1930s Villa is located at the top of Offa's Dyke, with views that are second to none. It is in e heart of the tranquil, historic estate and parkland of Chirk Castle Featuring a large rear terrace th seating area and lawned gardens, perfect for relaxing and admiring this spectacular countryside. e exterior is not Art Deco, being of the typical 30s villa but some of the rooms feature Deco irrors and small items of furniture. It has 3 bedrooms and sleeps 5 people. The property ference number is 008030 and it is owned by The National Trust for holiday lettings.

lilton Hotel

ngsway, Cardiff CF10 3HH
920 646409 www.hilton.com/cardiff

though the original steel framed structure was actually built in 1947, it is in the style of Art Deco. was the regional headquarters of the Prudential Assurance Company and is faced in brilliant rtland stone. It was purchased by Hilton Hotels in 1997. The architects Powell Dobson, mpathetically maintained much of the original stone façade. The focal point is provided by a glass of atrium which houses one of the largest ballrooms in the city. The furnishings and fittings roughout are opulent and in the Art Deco style – particularly the reception and foyer areas, with tures, fittings and furnishings all giving that 'wow' factor upon entering. The Hilton has the Razzi staurant and the Metropole Lounge both of which have very stylish décor. The 197 contemporary led bedrooms and suites are very comfortable, all with little deco touches.

Ardwyn House

ation Road, Llanwrtyd House, Powys LD5 4RW
591 610768 www.ardynhouse.co.uk

his delightful guest house was constructed between 1910 and 1920, and it still retains many of the iginal period features. It is a precursor to Art Deco being on the cusp of the transitional period d the Art Nouveau features are glorious. The classic Art Nouveau 'Tulip', 'Whiplash' and 'Rose' yles are repeated throughout the house. The bedrooms are tastefully decorated and all fixtures, tings and fabrics used in refurbishing over the years have always been in keeping with the property d selected to complement each area. The overall atmosphere in this haven is that of 'Belle oque' where the design and flair eclipses the darker Victorian era in anticipation of new things come.

he Hotel Portmerion

inffordd, Penrhyndeudraeth, Gwynedd LL48 6ER
766 770000 Architect Clough Williams-Ellis www.portmeironvillage.com

his hotel is set amongst the Portmeiron village which was built in two stages, from 1925-39 then 954-76, owing to the interception of WWII. The whole village is the work of Clough Williams-lis whose life long dream was to create a unique romantic village haven. His vision was to show ow a naturally beautiful site could be developed without spoiling it. His aim was also to hopefully ake people think about buildings in the landscape.

The jewel in the crown for this visually delightful hotel, is the 1931 built curvilinear dining room in typical Art Deco shape and design, inside and out this restaurant and Hotel are a star attraction. The rest of the hotel is beautifully decorated in traditional and contemporary design.

It was in Portmerion that that most iconic of TV series, the Prisoner, starring Patrick McGoohan, was filmed in the 1960s.

WALES RESTAURANTS, BARS & CAFES

Portmerion Restaurant

Minffordd, Penrhyndeudraeth, Gwynedd LL48 6ER
1766 770000 www.portmeironvillage.com

The Port Meiron Restaurant which is part of The Hotel has a visually stunning dining room which was built by Clough Williams-Ellis in 1931, as a curvilinear extension to his main hotel, overlooking the estuary. The dining room was redesigned by Terence Conran in 2005, and it is beautifully and subtly decorated throughout. It is pure joy to feast your eyes on the surroundings without even sampling the scrumptious culinary delights.

Dylan's Restaurant

Maes y mor, Criccieth, Gwynedd LL52 0HU
1766 522773 Built 1954
Architect Clough Williams Ellis

This building looks like it has just stepped out of the art deco era with its curved shape and floor to ceiling windows with thick stone walls. In fact it was the same architect Clough Williams Ellis who created Portmeiron Village who also designed this building in such an individualistic art deco style.

It has had a colourful history, as one of its early owners was Sir Billy Butlin, who entertained holidaymakers by bringing them in by bus to enjoy tea dances. Following on from this era it has been host to clubs and cafes until 2015 when Dylan's Restaurant took it over and sympathetically refurbished the building. It is an absolute joy to look at, both inside and out and a wonderful setting for enjoying a jolly good meal and daydreaming about all those excitable holidaymakers 'tripping the light fantastic'.

Zerodegrees Restaurant

27 Westgate Street, Cardiff CF10 1DD
029 2022 9494

The beauty in this building is when you look up to see the Art Deco frieze, on the frontage of the building. You are rewarded with a stylised motor car and aeroplane from the inter-war period with "Carways" and "Airways" written above. The central emblem depicts wings and a car tyre behind a flaming torch. This building was originally constructed in the 1930s as a shared garage for the Queen's Hotel and the Royal Hotel. The latter still exists, a little to the south. Both these hotels catered for well travelled guests, and the bold confident use of Art Deco on the garage's exterior – as well as the plane picture – were intended to reinforce the idea of sophistication and modernity.

The garage was modern in its construction too, using concrete and a framework of steel. It remained in use as a garage, latterly for taxis, into the 21st century. In 2007-2008 it was converted into the restaurant and microbrewery. The brewing equipment takes pride of place beside the windows.

Le Monde Restaurant

60-62 St Mary Street, Cardiff CF10 1FE
029 2038 7376

This restaurant is housed in a nineteenth century warehouse and has a very pleasant and elegant art deco style interior.

The Palladium

Wetherspoons Pub/Restaurant,
7 Gloddaeth Street, Llandudo LL30 2DD
01492 863920
1920 Architect Arthur Hewitt

The exterior of this previous cinema is built and decorated predominantly in the Georgian style, but it is the interior which has the art deco features. The elaborate wood panelling, ornate detailing on the walls and ceilings along with the 'must visit' powder rooms (lavatories) are all a feast for your eyes.

Waterloo Tearoom

1-3 Washington Buildings, Stanwell Road, Penarth, Vale of Glamorgan CF64 2AD
029 2070 9158

This modern interior designed tea house is located in a listed Art Deco frontage building, which used to house the Washington Cinema from the 1930s. It is very pleasing to be able to enjoy the striking exterior then sample some very select teas whilst day dreaming about the past events that took place in such a special building.

WALES THEATRES & CINEMAS

enarth Pier Pavillion

e Esplanade, Penarth CF64 3AU
920 712100 info@penarthpavilionpier.co.uk

narth is a lovely town in the Vale of Glamorgan, just over 5 miles south west from the city centre
Cardiff. It is positioned on the north shore of the Severn Estuary. The impressive Pavilion
corporates a community cinema, retail area, café, bar, and restaurant. The Pavilion has been
mpathetically restored to highlight its amazing Art Deco architecture. It is an iconic mark on the
dscape and the silver grey capped twin towered and curvilinear Pavilion with lattice work are a
y to encounter.

ew Theatre

rk Place, Cardiff CF10 3LN
9 2087 8889 Built 1904 Architects Runtz & Ford

is glorious Theatre was built pre Deco times but was a
rerunner of the architectural style to come. It has a
autiful rounded exterior to the building, which is made
of brick and Bath stone. The interior is not a
sappointment as all areas are richly decorated, and
ulently carpeted with the dress circle, orchestra and
cony areas all being luxuriously upholstered in crimson
vet. A tasteful and highly decorated mural is displayed in
eam and gold on the dress circle. This famous 1,570
ating theatre has seen the likes of legendary jazz pianist
ly Roll Morton in 1923. During 1931 some structural
erations were made to allow the showing of films.

Newbridge Memo

High Street, Newbridge, Gwent NP11 4FH
01495 243252 Built 1924

Now known as the Newbridge Memo, the Memorial Hall is part of the Celynen Collieries Institut
& Memorial buildings, which are grade II listed. The building opened in 1908 as a lasting monumen
to the miners and the Memorial Hall, built in 1924, serves as a memorial to the local servicemen
who lost their lives during WW1.

The Hall auditorium was unusual for its time as the forward thinking planners decided to combin
theatre and cinema with a ballroom underneath.

Traditionally theatres had seating boxes around the proscenium arch and curved rows of seatin
but this would have been unsuitable for cinemas as the images projected need to be viewed fla
The Memo auditorium was designed without curved seating or boxes, allowing it to be versatil
with the times. Another concession was that the 'fly floor' or gallery which is used to provide
working platform for raising and lowering the cloth scenery was located to one side instead
centrally, demonstrating that it was built as a professional dual purpose stage.

The auditorium has an opulent sense of decadent Art Deco grandeur that creates a wonderful
romantic and nostalgic atmosphere. The flamboyant proscenium arch with its gilded bead and re
acanthus and Greek key mouldings are a mighty focal point above the stage. It was certainly fittin
for the first film, which was shown in the Hall in 1925, that of 'The Thief of Baghdad' starring no
other than Rudolph Valentino. Music has also played an important role in the Memo and th
recently refurbished auditorium once again has bought creativity and vitality back into th
community with a variety of events, daily classes and evening entertainment.

WALES LIDOS

ey rose like the 'fountain of youth' in all their glory during the 1920s and 30s when health experts ped the mix of fresh air and exercise they offered might help counter conditions like tuberculosis ich was then common in Wales's industrial landscape.

rprisingly Wales had more than 50 lidos, varying in size and design which were built and dotted ound the heartlands. Many were architectural 'Goddesses' of the Art Deco era which sat badly with e harsh reality of the grime and dirt of the local coalmining industries. In their time, they were mensely popular, but with the advent of WWII and the subsequent aftermath, many sadly fell into srepair.

e remaining Lidos then became ss frequented, due to the popularity holidaying further afield and the se in cheap foreign travels of the 60s and 70s. Today, only one mains and that is Pontypridd Lido hich is the sole survivor. I know of any hard working campaigners hose love for the lost lidos never lls. They are busy promoting the lue of our past architectural eritage and raising much needed nds to breathe new life into these prious and functional pleasure oases.

© Rhondda Cynon Taf Council

Pontypridd Lido

nysangharad Park, Pontypridd, Rhondda Cynon Taf
uilt 1927

llowing a major restoration, at a cost of 6.3 million pounds this magnificent Lido is set to open in 15. Funding was raised through Rhondda Cynon Taf Council with financial support from the ropean Regional Development Fund via the Welsh Government, and the Heritage Lottery Fund.

is such an exciting time as this arts and crafts style lido was built with a Mediterranean influence and its heyday it could accommodate up to 1000 people. It has been fully restored in all its glory and

sympathetically remodelled with three heated swimming pools to offer a varied facility for all age groups.

It includes a café, modern play area and heated changing facilities. The original turnstiles and wooden cubicles have been fully restored. There is also a permanent display depicting the history of the lido and a wider area for educations purposes.

WALES PLACES OF INTEREST

Cardiff Central Railway Station

The Esplanade, Penarth CF64 3AU
02920 712100 info@penarthpavilionpier.co.uk

If you arrive in Cardiff by train you will not be disappointed with the station that greets you. T
Great Western Railway, which built the current station buildings from 1932 to 1934, consists

lovely details from the 193
rebuild which include the cupc
with its large clock, and the w
tiles, including the hands pointi
from the subway to th
platforms. The Art Deco lamps
the booking hall are replicas
the originals, installed in 19
with funding from the Railw
Heritage Trust, and a
wonderful.
Well worth taking a meand
along to see.

Newport Civic Centre

Newport, South Wales NP20 4UR
Opened 1964 Architect Thomas Cecil Howitt

This grade II listed building is in the Art Deco style and stands magnificently and majestically in th
centre of Newport. Even though it is post deco period in date, it was magnificently designed in th
Art Deco style.

Newport City Live Arena

Clarence Place, Newport, Gwent NR19 7AB   01633 213344
1938 Architect Harry Weedon

Originally opened as an Odeon cinema the
unmistakable art deco style of Harry Weedon
is plain to see here. This large grade II listed
building is now home to a lively venue which
hosts staged music performances and acts
along with a huge screen which shows live
sporting events. It could so easily have been
demolished after it fell derelict, but fortunately
after being purchased by a local Business
couple, it was reborn again following over a
one million pound investment.

wansea Guildhall

ansea SA1 4PE
ilt 1934 Architect Sir Percy Thomas

e Guildhall is the main building for the City and County of Swansea Council. Construction began
1930 and was completed 4 years later. It was considered somewhat controversial at the time
it was representative of the modern movement in architecture and was described as having a
ripped classical' style (a follow-on from the ornate buildings of the 19C being less ornate and
pler in design). The Portland stone exterior and tall art deco clock tower stand proudly, making
a local landmark for all to enjoy.

emple of Peace and Health

thays Park, Cardiff CF10 3AP
ilt 1937-38 Architect Sir Percy Thomas

e (Welsh National) Temple of Peace and Health is a non-religious civic building. It is built in the
rman/Italianate public building style and is a bold striking modern building. The building is in the
m of the letter 'T', and it has two wings either side made out of Portland stone. The roofs of
e wings are dark red Italian pattern tiles. Incorporated in the building are different materials
m various countries to emphasise the international nature of the work carried out inside the
ilding. The entrance hall and vestibule has large pillars as you enter and behind these columns
portico are three magnificent windows which have panels above depicting figures which
present Health, Justice and Peace.
e Temple Hall is lined with dove-grey marble to symbolise the emblem of Peace.

Credits & Acknowledgments

I would like to thank my Editor Richard N. Wilthew for his ongoing support and expertise of whi I am deeply indebted.

All the kind and helpful people at the hotels, restaurants, lidos etc. who have given up their time assist me in completing this book; to name just a few:

The Press team at Claridges Hotel, Corbin & King, Eddie Gershon at JD Wetherspoons, Dav Webb for his photographs, Lesley at the Grand Hotel Glasgow, Sue at The Arlington, Tricity Vog for being absolutely amazing and James Millar for some super photographs.

The National Trust, English Tourist Board and English Heritage of whom have all been very c operative and obliging.

Lisa at Vintage Life Magazine and the team at Best of British Magazine.

Crispin de Boos at Erskine Press.

All at Barkers Print & Design.

Useful web pages for your further enjoyment:

www.vintagelifemagazine.com

www.nationaltrust.org.uk

www.bestofbritishmag.co.uk

www.english-heritage.org.uk

www.sinbozkurtshop.com

www.tricityvogue.com

www.visitbritain.com

www.jamesmillar.co.uk

www.lottiedavis.com

www.champagnecharliemusic.co.uk

Any further information can be obtained at
www.artdecopublisher@hotmail.com

Modern Revival of the Jazz Age

ver the past ten years we have gratefully seen a steady increase in the performing arts and musical ents dedicated to the 1920s and 30s era. The risqué but beautiful art of Burlesque has surrected itself in the most respectable venues across Britain, live swing, jazz and blues are readily ailable and a large, ever increasing following of all ages, for all things vintage are attending festivals e Twinwood in Bedfordshire, the Goodwood Revival in Sussex and the Morecambe Vintage stival. They are proving so popular that tickets get sold out as soon as they are released.

is these talented and dedicated artists who have helped to revive and inspire future generations good old fashioned entertainment values. How nice it is to hear every word that is sung, and be part of an establishment of well behaved but fun loving entertainers like Champagne Charlie d Tom Carradine.

usical Director and Pianist Tom Carradine is a ented dapper chappie. Versatility is his name and compliments the 1920s and 30s era with his usical prowess, adapting from suave sophistication

city Vogue

Sin Bozkurt

©James Millar

to the very jaunty Cockney Sing-a-Long! Three cheers for Mr Carradine, the Musical Hall and Cabaret artist aficionado.

Proper dancing takes time and patience but is very rewarding; you feel that you have achieved something when eventually your two left feet do as they are told! Hurray to 'Melody Man' a regular on the circuit from the Bedfordshire Lindy Hop Group who has been the inspiration for many to take up dancing. Mark and Hoc tirelessly go through the paces year in and out to instil confidence in the all ages up and down the country to take their first dance steps.

A master compare and cabaret act is the tantalising Dusty Limits who regularly appears at Cabaret Clubs in London's top Hotels and at the annual Twinwood festival. If you have not had the pleasure of seeing the luscious Lola Lamour an accomplished singer who performs with the Blue Light Boys and the Lamours this is a must.

Lola can be found at many venues across Britain and attends many of the 1940s events and major festivals.

It is the hard work and passion of these artists and many more at home and abroad who keep alive our musical and artistic heritage whilst adding their own twist, which has set the ball rolling for an ever increasing revival of nostalgia entertainment.

If you are lucky enough to be at one of the all girl band Tricity Vogues' performances you will not be disappointed. The energetic talented group put on such a visual and musical feast you are immediately transported right back to the Gatsby era.

©Lottie Davi

Saving our Art Deco heritage

Having travelled extensively over the years for business and leisure I have felt privileged and honoured to have slept in, dined at, drank in, swam in, and laughed in, some of our most phenomenal 20th century architecture. To have sat on the most exquisite art deco furniture and drank from striking coffee cups, art deco touches every nuance of our lives.

No architectural movement or style has had such an effect on so many people and objects before or after. It is unique and that is why we have to preserve, and restore our 20th century heritage for future generations to enjoy.

I am always saddened to hear that a place I have visited has been demolished to make way for a new supermarket or that is it too expensive to upkeep despite local outcry.

I am also always euphoric when I hear that a Peoples Trust or organisation has been formed and that a plan has been drawn up to raise the profile of the Cinema (Regent Centre, Christchurch, Dorset) indoor Swimming Pool (Bon Accord Baths in Aberdeen), Lido (Saltdean Lido Brighton), to save it from dereliction and ultimate oblivion.

I urge any person who has a passion for Art Deco to seek out your nearest monument and support it by using it, as it is no good just to save these iconic buildings, they need to be patronised to keep them viable. If like Saltdean Lido in Brighton the 'phoenix is rising' then support the ongoing campaigns by attending fundraising events or offering your time as a volunteer as the life long rewards you will reap will outweigh any downsides.

My hat goes off (and I have many!) to all you dedicated and hardworking people who often go unrecognised, we all owe you our wholehearted gratitude for helping to save our iconic art deco heritage. Thank You.

Friends of Bude Sea Pool

INDEX

LONDON

HOTELS

10	Claridge's
12	The Dorchester
14	The May Fair
16	Savoy
19	Strand Palace
19	The Wellesley
20	The Beaumont
22	The Ritz
26	Thistle Marble Arch
27	Park Lane Hotel
28	Town Hall Hotel & Apartments
28	Hotel 41
29	Waldorf Hilton
30	Imperial

RESTAURANTS, BARS & CAFES

18	Kaspars Bar & Grill
23	The Palm Court
25	Rivioli Bar
28	Palm Court Bar
29	Homage Restaurant
29	Good Godfrey's Bar & Lounge
30	Bibendum Restaurant
32	Brasserie Zedel
34	OXO Tower Restaurant
34	The Wolseley
35	Oscar's Bar & Restaurant at Charlotte Street Hotel

DORCHESTER RESTAURANTS

34	Bar 45
35	The Grill
35	Cut
36	China Tang

SAVOY RESTAURANTS

37	Savoy Grill
37	American Bar
38	Kaspar's Bar & grill
38	Beaufort Bar
39	Thames Foyer

CLARIDGES RESTAURANT

39	Fera

WELLESLEY RESTAURANTS

40	The Crystal Bar
40	The Oval

THE BEAUMONT RESTAURANTS

40	Colony Grill Room
41	American Bar

PARK LANE HOTEL RESTAURANTS

41	The Palm Court Bar & Lounge

THE RITZ RESTAURANTS

42	Rivoli Bar
43	The Palm Court

WALDORF HILTON RESTAURANTS

43	Good Godfrey's Bar & Lounge
44	Bob Bob Ricard
45	Quaglino's
45	Fischer's
46	Boulestin
47	Berners Tavern
47	Massimo Restaurant & Oyster Bar

HOTEL CAFÉ ROYAL RESTAURANT

48	The Café
49	Ten Room
49	O.W.B.
49	Black Cat Cabaret
50	The Domino
50	The Delaunay
50	Sketch
51	Kettner's Bar
51	Patisserie Valeerie
51	E Pellicci Café
52	Le QuecumBar & Brasserie
52	The Night Jar
53	Floridita
53	Experimental Cocktail Club
53	Colbert
54	Le Deux Salons

THEATRES & CINEMAS

55	Prince Edward Theatre
56	Apollo Victoria Cinema
56	Adelphi Theatre
56	Prince of Wales Theatre
57	The Odeon, Leicester Square
57	Odeon Cinema Muswell Hil
58	Everyman Cinemas
59	Troxy
60	Vue Cinema
60	Phoenix Cinema
61	The Rio Cinema
61	Watford Colosseum
61	Wilton's Music Hall

LIDOS

62	Brockwell Lido
63	Charlton Lido
63	Tooting Bec Lido
63	Hampton Open Air Pool
64	Hillingdon Sports & Leisure Complex
64	Park Road Pools
64	London Fields Lido
65	Oasis Swimmimg Pools
65	Parliament Hill Lido
66	Ruislip Lido
66	The Serpentine Lido

PLACES OF INTEREST

68	Oxo Tower
69	Adelaide House
70	Daily Express Newspaper office
70	BBC Broadcasting House
71	Selfridges
71	National Audit Office
71	Abbey National Building Society
71	Shell-Mex Co. Building
72	Barkers Department Store
72	Battersea Power Station
72	London Underground Headquarters
72	Hoover Building ,Perivale
73	London Zoo
73	Palladium House
73	Carreras Cigarette Factory
74	Eltham Palace London
74	Florin Court
75	Art Deco Underground Stations
76	Isokon Building

ACCOMMODATION

Norwich	Norfolk	St Giles House Hotel
Old Hunstanton	Norfolk	Little Stints Holiday Apartment
Sheringham	Norfolk	Seaspray House
Northampton		The Aviator Hotel
Saltdean	Sussex	Bethany Art Deco House
Arundel	W. Sussex	Manor Road Garagew – The Pit Stop
Margate	Kent	Walpole Bay Hotel
Margate	Kent	Pink House
Seaview	Isle of Wight	Priory Bay Hotel
Walsingham	Norfolk	Control Tower B & B
Lenham	Kent	Who'd A Thought It
Brighton	E Sussex	Paskins Hotel
Whitstable	Kent	Hotel Continental
Weybridge	Surrey	Brooklands Hotel
Minster	Kent	Holiday Inn Express
Horley	Surrey	Springwood Guest House
Birchington	Kent	Whitehouse B & B
St Osyth	Essex	Old Cafe Holiday Home
Hatfield	Hertfordshire	Ramada Hotel
Farnborough	Hampshire	Aviator Hotel

RESTAURANTS, BARS CAFES

St Albans	Hertfordshire	Cafe Rouge
Brighton	Sussex	Metrodeco
Maidstone	Kent	Embankments Bar & Restaurant
Stortford	Hertfordshire	Nags Head Pub
Cambridge		Regal Restaurant
Norwich	Norfolk	Jamie's Italian
Norwich	Norfolk	Marmalades Cafe
Whitstable	Kent	The Peter Cushing Restaurant & Pub
Southend	Essex	Arlington Ballroom
Littlehampton	W Sussex	East Beach Cafe

THEATRES & CINEMAS

King's Lynn	Norfolk	Majestic Cinema
Fakenham	Norfolk	Hollywood Cinema
Bexhill on Sea	E Sussex	The De La Warr Pavillion
St Albans	Hertfordshire	Odyssey Cinema
Cambridge		Arts Picture House
Berkhamsted	Hertfordshire	Rex Cinema
Christchurch	Dorset	Regent Centre
Worthing	E Sussex	Assembly Hall
Letchworth	E Sussex	Broadway Cinema
Cromer	Norfolk	Regal Movieplex
Sandwich	Kent	Empire Cinema
Margate	Kent	Theatre Royal
Watford	Watford	Colosseum
Clacton-on-Sea	Essex	Princes Theatre
Clacton-on-Sea	Essex	Century Cinema

LIDOS

Brighton	E Sussex	Saltdean Lido
Tollesbury	Essex	Woodup Outdoor Amenity Pool
Woburn	Bedfordshire	Woburn Open Air Swimming Pool
Ware	Hertfordshire	Priory Lido
Lewes	East Sussex	Pells Outdoor
Letchworth	Hertfordshire	Letchworth Open Air Pool
Hitchin	Hertfordshire	Hitchin Swimming Pool
High Wycombe	Bucks	Wycombe Rye Park
Gillingham	Kent	Strand Leisure Park
Guilford	Surrey	Guilford Lido
Cambridge		Jesus Green Lido

PLACES OF INTEREST

105	Norwich	Norfolk	City Hall
105	Norwich	Norfolk	Royal Arcade
106	Norwich	Norfolk	Bridewell Museum
106	Norwich	Norfolk	Deco Days
106	Holt	Norfolk	Baron Art
107	Debenham	Suffolk	Deco Debenham
107	Hunstanton	Norfolk	
107	Wisbech	Cambridgeshire	Empire Theatre
107	Letchworth	Hertfordshire	The Spirelli Building
108	Margate	Kent	Dreamland Amusement Park
108	Margate	Kent	Dreamland Cinema
109	Cliftinville	Kent	Palm Bay Avenue
109	Margate	Kent	Margate Museum
109	Shoreham	W Sussex	Shoreham Airport
109	Wisbech	Norfolk	Princes Canning Factory
109	Worthing	W Sussex	Worthing Pier
110	Worthing	W Sussex	Stoke Abbot Court
110	Worthing	W Sussex	Onslow Court Apartments
110	Brighton	E Sussex	Embassy Court
111	St Leonards	E Sussex	Marine Court
111	Esher	Surrey	The Homewood
112	Brentford	Middlesex	JC Decaux
112	Maidstone	Kent	Leeds Castle

SOUTH WEST

ACCOMMODATION

114	Bigbury-on-Sea	Devon	Burgh Island Hotel
116	Shanklin	Isle of Wight	Marine Villa
117	West Wittering	W Sussex	Turritella
117	Weymouth	Dorset	Portland House
118	Wadebridge	Cornwall	St Moritz Hotel
119	Braunton	Devon	Saunton-Sands Hotel
120	Lizard Peninsula	Cornwall	Mullion Cove Hotel
120	Weymouth	Dorset	Riviera Hotel
121	Bournemouth	Dorset	Cumberland Hotel
122	St Leonards	Gloucester	Mercure Bowden Hall
123	Bournemouth	Dorset	Premier Inn
123	St Ives	Cornwall	Seaspray House
124	Lymington	Hampshire	Tower Hall B&B
124	Dartmouth	Devon	Kaywana Hall B & B
125	Falmouth	Cornwall	Beach House B & B
126	Southsea	Hampshire	The Ferryman B & B
126	Penzance	Cornwall	The Yacht Inn
126	Torquay	Devon	Queens Quay
127	Torquay	Devon	The Corbyn Apartments
127	Bristol	Mercure	Brigstow Hotel

RESTAURANTS, BARS CAFES

128	Helston	Cornwall	Glenbevrie Bar
128	Bristol		Hyde & Co Bar
129	Bath		Bea's Vintage Tea Room
129	Gloucester		Regal Restaurant & Bar
129	Cheltenham	Gloucester	The Daffodil
130	Leamington Spa	Warwickshire	Bill's Cafe & Restaurant
130	Bovey	Devon	Bovey Castle Hotel
131	Torquay	Devon	Harvester Restaurant

CINEMAS & THEATRES

132	Bristol		Odeon & UCI Cinema
132	Bristol		Everyman Cinema
132	Eversham	Gloucestershire	Regal Cinema
133	St Ives	Cornwall	Royal Cinema

3	Penzance	Cornwall	Savoy Cinema
4	Redruth	Cornwall	Regal Cinema & Theatre
4	Illfracombe	Devon	Embassy Cinema
5	Tiveton	Devon	Tivoli Cinema
5	Wellington	S Somerset	Wellesley Cinema
5	Exeter		Odeon Cinema
6	Barnstaple	Devon	Scott Cinema
6	Bridgewater	Somerset	Scott Cinema
6	Lyme Regis	Dorset	Scott Cinema
7	Axbridge	Somerset	Roxy Community Cinema
8	Clevedon	Nth Somerset	Curzon Community Cinema
8	Weston-s.-Mare	Somerset	Odean Cinema
9	Torquay	Devon	Babbacombe

LIDOS

0	Wiveliscombe	Somerset	Wiveliscombe Open Air Pool
0	Stroud	Gloucestershire	Stratford Park Leisure Centre
0	Street	Somerset	Greenback Swimming Pool
1	Lymington	Hampshire	Lymington Seawater Baths
1	Lydney	Gloucestershire	Bathurst Swimming Pool
1	Oxford		Hinksey Pool
1	Newton Abbot	Devon	Ashburton Open Air
2	Bude	Cornwall	Bude Sea Pool
2	Penzance	Cornwall	Jubilee Pool
3	Shepton Mallet	Somerset	Shepton Mallet Outdoor Pool
3	Newbuet	Berkshire	Northcroft Leisure Centre
3	Plymouth	Devon	Tinside Lido
3	Portsmouth	Hampshire	Hilsea Lido

PLACES OF INTEREST

5	Bornemouth	Dorset	House of Fraser
5	Bournemouth	Dorset	Beales Department Store
6	Bournemouth	Dorset	Bournemouth Pavilion
6	Bournemouth	Dorset	Bournemouth Daily Echo Bldg
6	Kingswear	Devon	Coleton Fishacre
7	Brixham	Devon	Greenway House
7	Redruth	Cornwall	La Belle Art Deco

AST MIDLANDS

ACCOMMODATION

9	Alvaston	Darby Derby	Conference Centre
9	Birmingham		53 & 54 Inge Street
0	Lincoln		Charlotte House Hotel

RESTAURANTS, BAR CAFES

1	Derby		Nando's
1	Alvaston	Derby	Blue Peter
2	Derby		Michael Frith at Bennetts
2	Ilkeston	Derbyshire	The General Havelock
3	West Bridgford	Nottingham	The Test Match Pub
3	Derby		Bean Caffe
4	Derby		Cosmo Restaurant

THEATRES & CINEMAS

5	Bradford	W Yorkshire	Pictureville Cinema
5	Melton Mowbray	Leicestershire	Regal Cinema
7	Nottingham		Savoy Cinema
7	Leicester		Athena Venue

LIDOS

8	Skegness	Lincolnshire	Embassy Outdoor Pool
8	Woodhall Spa	Lincolnshire	Woodhall Spa Swimming Pool
8	Bourne	Lincolnshire	Bourne Outdoor Pool
8	Hope Valley	Derbyshire	Hathersgate Open Air Pool

| 159 | Derby | | Queen's Leisure Centre |
| 159 | Upper Mounts | Northampton | Mounts Baths |

PLACES OF INTEREST

160	Derby		Natwest Bank
160	Worcester		Austin House
161	Derby		Market Place
161	Radford	Nottingham	Mount Zion Church
162	Derby		Co-operative Dept. Store
162	Northampton		78 Derngate Street

WEST MIDLANDS

ACCOMMODATION

165	Birmingham		Edgebaston Hotel
165	Birmingham		Holiday Inn
165	Coleshill	Birmingham	Grimscote Manor Hotel
166	Leamington Spa	Warwickshire	Mallory Court Hotel

BARS CAFES RESTAURANTS

167	Stratford-Upon-Avon		Rooftop Restaurant
167	Birmingham		Centenary Lounge Cafe
168	Greater Manchester		Brown's
169	Birmingham		The Grill Room

THEATRES & CINEMAS

170	Tenbury Wells	Worcestershire	Regal Cinema
170	Eversham	Worcestershire	Regal Cinema
171	Birmingham		Everyman Birmingham
171	Bridgenorth	Shropshire	Majestic Cinema
172	Birmingham		The Electric Cinema
172	Stoke-on-Trent	Staffordshire	Regent Theatre
172	Sutton Coldfield	W Midlands	Empire Cinema

LIDOS

173	Worcester		Droitwich Spa
173	Cheltenham	Gloucestershire	Sandford Park Lido
173	Birmingham		Moseley Road Baths

PLACES OF INTEREST

175	Worcester		Grays of Worcester
175	Kingstanding	Birmingham	Mecca Bingo
176	Birmingham		Barber Institute of Fine Arts
176	Liverpool		Co-operative Supermarket
177	Banbury	Warwickshire	Upton House & Gardens
177	Birmingham		Symphony Hall
178	Leicester		Athena Entertainment Centre

NORTH EAST

ACCOMMODATION

180	Breadnell	Northumberland	The Haven Beach
180	Newcastle-Upon-Tyne		Sandman Signature Hotel
180	Leeds		The Queens Hotel
181	Leeds		Radisson Blu Hotel
181	Tynemouth	North Shields	Park Hotel
181	Sheffield		Staindrop Lodge Hotel
181	Doncaster		The Earl of Doncaster
182	Skipton	N Yorkshire	Black Horse Hotel
182	Darlington		Holiday Inn
182	Hartlepool		The Staincliffe Hotel
182	Sunderland		Marriot Hotel
183	Newcastle-Upon-Tyne		Malmaison Hotel
183	Upper Swalesdale	Yorkshire	Rowland End Guest House
183	Bridlington	Yorkshire	Expanse Hotel

RESTAURANTS BARS CAFES

4	Whitley Bay	Tyne & Wear	Rendezvous Cafe
4	Newbiggin	Northumberland	Cafe Bertorelli
4	Scarborough	North Yorkshire	Francis Tea Room
5	Bradford		City Vaults Restaurant
5	Halifax	W Yorkshire	The Three Pigeons
5	Blyth	Northumberland	The Wallow
5	Newcastle-Upon Tyne		Malmaison Brasserie
5	Lincoln		The Ritz

THEATRES & CINEMAS

6	Newcastle-Upon-Tyne		Tyneside Cinema
6	Harrogate		Harrogate Odeon
6	Harrogate		Ritz Cinema & Theatre
6	Leeds		Hyde Park Picture House
7	Redcar	Cleveland	The Regent Cinema
8	Sheffield		Showroom Cinema & Cafe
8	Scarborough	N Yorkshire	Stephen Joseph Theatre
8	Alnwick	Northumberland	The Playhouse

LIDOS

9	Ilkley	W Yorkshire	Ilkley Pool & Lido
9	Ingleton	N Yorkshire	Ingleton Open Air Pool
0	Hathersage	Derbyshire	Hathersage Opne Ait Pool

PLACES OF INTEREST

1	Newcastle		Baltic Centre for Contemporary Arts
1	Newcastle		Wills Building
2	Newcastle		Co-op Building
2	Newcastle		The Central Lofts
2	Newcastle		Carliol House
2	Harrogate	N Yorkshire	The Sun Pavilion
3	Newport	Lincoln	Radio Lincolnshire Building
3	Cleethorpes	Lincolnshire	Electricity Board Showrooms
3	Sheffield		Central Library & Graves Gallery
4	Seaton Carew	Hartlepool	West Hartlepool Bus Station
4	Bede	Durham	The Chapel
4	Hartlepool		Hartlepool's Maritime Heitage

ORTH WEST

ACCOMMODATION

6	Morecombe	Lancashire	The Midland Hotel
7	Liverpool		Crown Plaza Hotel
7	Manchester		The Palace Hotel
8	Liverpool		Britannia Adelphi Hotel
9	Bradford	W Yorkshire	The Great Victoria Hotel
9	Wirral	Mersyside	Leverhulme Hotel
0	Fleetwood	Lancashire	North Euston Hotel
1	Blackpool		The Corona Hotel
1	Manchester		Gotham Hotel

RESTAURANTS BARS AND CAFES

2	Morecombe	Lancashire	Brucciani's Ice Cream Parlour
2	Preston	Lancashire	Brucciani's Cafe
2	Manchester		The Fitzgerald
2	Stockport		The Stockport Plaza
3	Blackpool		Parks Art Deco Cafe
3	Blackpool		Notarianni Brothers Ice Cream Parlour
3	Morecombe	Lancashire	Midland Hotel Restaurant
3	Morecombe	Lancashire	Winter Gardens

THEATRES & CINEMAS

| 4 | Fleetwood | Lancashire | Marine Hall |
| 4 | Cleveleys | Lancashire | Thornton Little Theatre |

205	Southport	Lancashire	Southport Little Theatre
205	Redford	Nottingham	Majestic Theatre
205	Greater Manchester		Stockport Plaza Cinema
206	Liverpool		Royal Court Theatre
206	Ambleside	Cumbria	Zeffirelli's Cinema & Restaurant
206	Chorley	Lancashire	Chorley Little Theatre
207	Liverpool		Plaza Community Cinema
207	Longridge	Lancashire	The Palace Theatre
207	Liverpool		Woolton Picture House
208	Liverpool		The Epstein Theatre
208	Morecombe	Lancashire	Winter Gardens

LIDOS

209	Crewe	Cheshire	Crewe Swimming Pool
210	Nantwich	Cheshire	Nantwich Lido
210	Northwich	Cheshire	Marbury Park Lido

PLACES OF INTEREST

211	Southport	Lancashire	Mecca Bingo
211	Salford	Manchester	AS Antique Galleries
211	Manchester		Dock Office
212	Manchester		House of Fraser
212	Manchester		The Trafford centre
213	Liverpool		Georges Dock Building
213	Liverpool		Philharmonic Hall
214	Liverpool		Littlewood's Building
214	Manchester		Assermbly Rooms of Jehovah's Witnesses
214	Morecombe	Lancashire	Marine Road Central

SCOTLAND

ACCOMMODATION

216	Glasgow		Grand Central Hotel
216	Glasgow		Beresford Serviced Apartments
217	Aberdeen		Aberdeen Northern Hotel
217	Aberdeen		Douglas Hotel
218	Glasgow		Blythswood Square Hotel
218	Oban	Argyll	The Regent Hotel
218	Edinburgh		The Scotsman Hotel
219	Inverness		The Drumossie Hotel
219	Inverness		Cnoc-na-Faire B & B
219	Auchterarder	Perthshire	Gleneagles
220	Crail Fife		Balcomie Links Hotel
220	Grantown-Spey	Invernesshire	Tigh na Sgaith Hotel
221	Oban		The Tin Church Catering Company

RESTAURANTS BARS CAFES

222	Glasgow	Willow Tea Rooms
222	Glasgow	Swing Bar
223	Glasgow	Variety Bar
223	Glasgow	Rogana Restaurant
223	Largs	Nardini's of Largs
223	Glasgow	The Steps Bar
224	Glasgow	Di Maggio's
224	Glasgow	Grosvenor Cinema & Cafe
224	Glasgow	Queens Cafe
224	Edinburgh	The White House Cafe
225	Edinburgh	Maybury Casino
225	Glasgow	The Dalon Restaurant
226	Aberdeen	Carron Art Deco Restaurant
226	Inchinnan	Royal Arch Bar
227	Edinburgh	Cafe St Honore

THEATRES & CINEMAS

8	Glasgow		Glasgow Film Theatre
8	Glasgow		Grosvenor Cinema & Cafe
8	Aberfeldy	Perthshire	Birks Cinema
9	Bathgate	W Lothian	Regal Cinema
9	Edinburgh		Dominion Cinema
0	St Andrews	Fife	The New Picture House
0	Bo'ness	W Lothian	The Hippodrome
0	Perth		The Playhouse IMAX Cinema
0	Aberdeen		Belmont Picture House
I	Campbeltown		The Picture House
I	Isle of Bute		Diascovery Centre Cinema

LIDOS

2	Stonehaven		Stonehaven Swimming Pool
2	Inverclyde		Gouroch Outdoor Pool
3	New Cumnoch	Ayrshire	New Cumnoch Open Air Pool
3	New Cumnoch	Ayrshire	The Trinkie

PLACES OF INTEREST

4	Glasgow		Luma Lamp Factory
5	Glasgow		St Andrew's House
5	Edinburgh		Greens Playhouse
5	Inverness		Castle Stuart Clubhouse
6	Glasgow		Ascot Cinema
6	Isle of Bute		Rothsay Pavilion
6	Girvan	South Ayrshire	Girvan Railway Hotel
6	Glasgow		The Vogue Bingo Hall

ALES

ACCOMMODATION

8	Swansea	The Grand Hotel
8	Llandudno	Escape Boutique B & B
8	Conwy	Quay Hotel and Spa
8	Gwynedd	Sunray Guest House
9	Wrexham	House by the Dyke
9	Cardiff	Hilton Hotel
9	Powys	Ardwyn House
9	Gwynedd	The Hotel Portmerion

RESTAURANTS BARS AND CAFES

I	Gwynedd	Portmerion Restaurant
I	Gwynedd	Dylan's Restaurant
2	Cardiff	Zerodegrees Restaurant
2	Cardiff	Le Monde Restaurant
2	Llandudno	The Palladium
2	Vale of Glamorgan	Waterloo Tearoom

THEATRES & CINEMAS

3	Penarth	Penarth Pier Pavillion
3	Cardiff	New Theatre
4	Gwent	Newbridge Memo

LIDOS

5	Pontypridd	Pontypridd Lido

PLACES OF INTEREST

6	Penarth	Cardiff Central Railway Station
6	Newport	Newport Civic centre
6	Newport	Newport City Live Arena
7	Swansea	Swansea Guildhall
7	Cardiff	Temple of Peace and Happiness